Erich von Däniken came to prominence in the 1970s
with his bestseller *Chariots of the Gods?* and has since written
many books on a similar theme. He continues his research
from his home in Switzerland and remains a passionate advocate
of the reality of extraterrestrial visits.

ERICH VON DÄNIKEN

ARRIVAL OF THE GODS

REVEALING THE ALIEN LANDING SITES OF NAZCA

Arrival of the Gods was first published 1997 as *Zeichen für die Ewigkeit* by C. Bertelsmann Verlag, an imprint of Verlagsgruppe Random House, Munich.

ISBN 1-84333-053-9

A catalogue record for this book is available from the British Library

Published in 2002 by
Vega
64 Brewery Road
London, N7 9NT

A member of the Chrysalis Group plc

Visit our website at www.chrysalisbooks.co.uk

Printed in China

DEC 1 1 2002

CONTENTS

FOREWORD

Nazca? What about it? We don't need to hear any more about *that*, do we?

Until a few years ago, I – like many others – thought I knew almost all there was to know about Nazca. I'm fully versed in all the specialist and popular literature on the subject, in all the theories and speculations. In the last 30 years I've been to Nazca countless times. I've spent weeks flying over the surrounding desert and the near hills, and at the beginning of the seventies I hiked and stumbled for days across the hot scree and the rust-brown stone. I thought I'd put my finger on the riddle of Nazca, but in the meantime it has dawned on me just how little I and everyone else actually know.

What on earth is Nazca? Above all it is mysterious and strange, even uncanny. Nazca is at the same time both understandable and opaque. It is magic, seductive, logical and absurd all at once. Nazca is like a thunderous assault on one's reason. Its message is veiled and confused – every single theory about it is contradictory. Nazca seems unfathomable and insoluble, crazy and senseless. Some of the 'scrape drawings', the visual messages surrounding the little town of Nazca, seem childish, the result of unthinking impulse; others seem to be appealing to our powers of reason, asking us to tease out the threads of this mystery and dig down to the truth.

Nazca has so far eluded the cleverest attempts to solve its riddle. This is perhaps not surprising, given the obstinate way human reason clings to what it already knows. In an almost obsessional way we transpose our ways of thinking and our knowledge onto people who lived long ago, and whose view of the world was quite different from ours. We believe our sharp, Sherlock Holmesian cunning, our scientific methodology, will lead us inevitably to the Holy Grail of knowledge. Or we follow a different, parapsychological route, and try to 'intuit' the truth about Nazca through some kind of supersensory perception, becoming dogmatic in the process: those who don't believe such 'truths' are almost guilty, it seems, of venal sin. So we have Nazca theories, Nazca speculations, Nazca dogmas, Nazca cloud-cuckooisms, and a host of other crazy commentaries about Nazca, which all, in the end, lead nowhere.

Nazca is gigantic – and I don't just mean its geographical dimensions. Like the Great Pyramid in Egypt, Nazca is a time machine that can transport us back to the past. Whoever grasps its significance gains a perspective of phenomenal depth, at the heart of which a mirror gleams and radiates light back up to the universe.

NAZCA, ON THE PAN-AMERICAN HIGHWAY

1

Those who don't like thinking should at least rearrange their prejudices from time to time.
LUTHER BURBANK, 1849–1926

O nce upon a time, over the hills and far away in Peru, there was a run-down, sleepy little village. It was linked to the great capital city of Lima only by a dust-road that no one travelled unless they absolutely had to, for it passed for hundreds of kilometres through an unrelenting desert of sand and boulders. Uphill, downhill, a curve here and there, and at last a short, perilous stretch of winding mountain pass. Every two hours or so one passed a tumbledown Indian village – always at a place where streams from the far Andes ran through on their way to the Pacific Ocean. At improvised stalls the Indians offered small, dark yellow bananas, oranges with tough peel, bright green lemons and home-brewed lemonades of all colours. The way of life of these villagers was modest and monotonous. Apart from fruit, they also planted carrots, potatoes, onions and cotton, and on Sundays they all gathered together in a small Catholic church.

Nowadays, half this route is a four-lane highway, the rest a broad, tarmac road. From Lima to Nazca is about 450 kilometres in a southerly direction, towards Chile via the world-famous Pan-American Highway. (Known in Europe as the Dream Road, it crosses the American continent from north to south, from Alaska to Chile.) The Indian villages along the route are still there but have grown enormously: traffic lights and one-way streets conduct the streams of traffic through townships bursting at the seams and saturated with exhaust fumes. Restaurants, petrol stations, bars and car repair workshops line the road.

1

[1]

Sleepy little Nazca has become a small town complete with museum, park, shops and banks. School attendance is compulsory. Hotels of varying quality compete with one another for the custom of tourists, long-distance drivers and adventurers. The streets are overhung with the usual advertising hoardings, and at the edge of town is a small aerodrome with a tower and bar. Between 100 and 150 US dollars buys Nazca addicts a flight over the world-famous Pampa de Nazca, and a good chance of throwing up as the pilots force their small machines out of one tight curve into another. After each half-hour excursion, every tourist receives a certificate from Aero Condor, signed and dated by the pilot, stating that he or she has flown over the Nazca plain.

And yet none of these hurried travellers gets a glimpse of the *real riddle* of Nazca. Why is that? The tourist flights concentrate mainly on the so-called 'scrape drawings' on the rust-brown surface of the desert. These depict such things as a giant spider,[1] a humming bird, a monkey, a spiral and a fish – all interspersed with ruler-straight,

2

narrow lines – and, on the slopes, various heads with rays radiating from them. There are also, finally, isolated markings on the ground which look like giant runways. All this can be observed only from an aeroplane. At ground level there is almost nothing to be seen.

I asked the chief pilot of Aero Condor, Eduardo Herran, why the tourists don't get to see the Ingenio valley and the mountains.

'We were advised to fly mainly over the scrape drawings, because these would be of interest to the tourists. The flights would also get too expensive if we were to buzz about all over the place for hours on end.'

I buzzed about all over the place – for days on end.

Flashback

In the spring of 1927, the Peruvian archaeologist Toribio Mejia Xesspe was working in a small side valley of the Rio de Nazca, where there were some pre-Inca ruins. As he climbed further up the slope, where he expected to find other such remains, he stopped to get his breath back and looked down upon the Pampa de Chiquerillo, the Pampa de los Chinos, and the Pampa de Nazca. Something seemed strange. In the black-brown desert below him he made out brighter, ruler-straight lines. But he did not think much more about them, assuming they were probably ancient, pre-Columbian trails. Not until 1940, after walking along two of the lines, did Toribio Mejia Xesspe write an article about his discoveries.[1] This was the first information to appear in print on the lines of Nazca.

On 22 June 1941, Dr Paul Kosok, historian at the Long Island University in New York, climbed aboard a single-engine plane to search for water canals between the villages of Ica and Nazca. He knew that the Incas and other tribes predating them had laid down water supply channels; these however always vanished from view at some point or other. He was hoping he would be able to pinpoint the ancient conduits more easily from the air. He had also known for two years that down there on the plain, somewhere between the Ingenio stream and the village of Nazca, lay strange lines that seemed to have been scraped out of the ground. He wondered whether the lines had anything to do with the water supply system.

The late afternoon was clear, like all other days in that region. Dr Kosok strained his eyes but saw only the rust-brown surface beneath him, until the aeroplane began to follow the winding road up towards Nazca. Suddenly, 3 kilometres from the bend which leads from the Ingenio valley to the plain of Nazca, Dr Kosok noticed two narrow, parallel lines in the dark-brown ground below. What could they be? Kosok asked the pilot to turn around and follow the lines. Starting from a hill, they stretched for 2 kilometres over the pampa, ending in what seemed to be a runway. Kosok estimated the strip to be 30 metres wide and at least a kilometre long. How could that be? Who on earth would have laid down an airstrip in this wilderness? Kosok became nervous and ordered the pilot to turn back. After flying in the opposite direction for a few minutes, the aeroplane passed over a perfect spiral lying next to a strip even broader than the previous one. One kilometre further south, Kosok caught sight of the outline of a bird with a wingspan of 200 metres, and yet another strip beside it. Excited, Kosok got the pilot to fly round and round, descending closer to the ground. He saw a giant spider, then the clear contours of a monkey with a curling tail. Upon a sheer cliff face was drawn a 29-metre-high human figure, hand outstretched in a gesture of greeting. And upon smaller hills were engraved faces crowned with wreaths of rays and with helmets. Dr Paul Kosok had accidentally discovered man's most mysterious picture book.[2, 3]

Once back on terra firma, Kosok asked the archaeologists what they thought. They knew nothing about what he had seen, but one thing was clear: the strips could not possibly be runways, since neither the Indians nor the Incas, let alone any pre-Inca tribes, had had flying machines! The lines were therefore designated as 'ancient Inca roads' or 'processional paths'. A theory about some curious kind of religion was even put forward to explain them. The Indian tribes had, after all, indulged in all sorts of strange magic rites.

Years passed. In the meantime, the German geographer and mathematician Maria Reiche (who had trained at Hamburg University and the Dresden Institute of Technology) travelled to Peru. She had no knowledge of the strange markings at Nazca, but was interested in the ruins of the Andes region. In particular she wanted to research the calendrical connections of the many Peruvian *Intihuantanas* or 'sun-watch sites'. Whether by chance or destiny, she met Paul Kosok, who told her with great excitement of the strange markings at Nazca. The young German, with her training and her knowledge of calendar relationships, struck Kosok as the perfect person to unlock the secret of Nazca.

In 1946, spurred on by Kosok, Maria Reiche began to turn her attention to this subject – initially alongside her other work. But she was soon spellbound by the fascinating markings. Beside the dusty road leading from the Ingenio valley to Nazca stood a modest *hacienda* or farm, and its owners allowed Reiche to rent a room there. A room in the Hacienda San Pablo thus became this tireless young woman's research headquarters for a good number of years. Today, in the nearby Museo Maria Reiche, there is a waxwork figure of her at work, surrounded by maps and drawings.[2] The other rooms in the museum contain impressive black-and-white photographs from this time.

Maria Reiche's first step was to get some sort of overview of the confusion of lines on the desert surface. Armed with a straw hat and a

[2]

drawing pad, she wandered around in the fierce heat, staking out the terrain and making the first drawings. She soon realized that aerial photographs would be indispensable. Acquaintances of hers helped her make contact with the Servicio Aerofotographico Nacional, a branch of the Peruvian airforce. Its pilots and officers were not only interested in her work, but also very eager to help – and so the first aerial photographs and measurements were taken.

Distortions and subversions!

In the mid-fifties, Maria Reiche herself compared the trail-like lines with a landing strip. She later mentioned this in her booklet *Geheimnis der Wüste* (Secret of the Desert):[4]

> Looking down from the plane upon the flat surface of the desert, the traveller will discover, etched into the high terraces and slopes, gigantic triangles and squares whose outlines look as though they have been drawn with a ruler, and whose light surfaces contrast clearly with the dark ground. *One could almost believe they were airstrips!* [my italic].

In 1968 – before Reiche's book had appeared – when I said more or less the same thing in my book *Erinnerungen an die Zukunft* (Chariots of the Gods?),[5] I was torn apart. What a sin I had committed! Let me cite the offending passage:

> The 60-kilometre-long plain of Nazca, seen from the air, has the undoubted look of an airport – Is it really too far-fetched to suggest that lines were laid down here to give the message to the gods: 'Land here! Everything has been prepared as you ordained it!' Did the architects of these lines know what they were doing? Did they perhaps know what the 'gods' needed in order to be able to land?

Since I wrote these few lines, published nearly 30 years ago but written two years before that, a host of statements which I have *never* published, written or spoken have been wrongly attributed to me. Luckily I do not suffer from a persecution complex, nor do I subscribe to conspiracy theories. But it does give cause for concern when 'serious' media and 'scientific' publications disseminate unfounded nonsense. The way I have been misconstrued is a textbook example of how falsely interpreted statements get carved in stone and filed in press archives to be falsely cited again at every opportunity. Young Erich von Däniken wrote in 1966 that, seen from the air, the plain of Nazca looks like a landing strip. But the young Maria Reiche said the same thing for heaven's sake!

At the same time, the whole scientific press and all the scientific publications that I know of – and that's quite a few, I can tell you – assure the world in tones of honest indignation that I have said the Nazca plain was once a 'landing station' for spaceships. Here is one example from a more recent scientific magazine:[6]

> At the beginning of the seventies, a certain Erik [with a k!] von Däniken announced that the lines were landing strips for spaceships. His pseudo-proofs were pictures of geoglyphs with a startling similarity to modern airstrips. He added that it was impossible to create such large signs and markings without the help of aeroplanes.

The scientific literature is full of such bath-tub toys purporting to be truth. Not only have none of these clever writers read the book in question – let alone the ones which followed,[7-9] instead copying down nonsense from each other – but they also maliciously invent and attribute to me things which cannot be found anywhere in any of my books. So you will understand if I, for my part, do not take these 'scientific' journalists and authors seriously! 'Success is about the last thing you're forgiven for' (Truman Capote).

Anyway, once the Peruvian airforce had offered support to Maria Reiche, the Ministry of Education also provided modest help. Later on, the American Wenner-Gren Foundation and the German Research Society also contributed to the project. In the following years, other institutions made further small amounts of funding available. There was too little for a large-scale research project, but enough to carry on the work. Undaunted, Maria Reiche hauled a 2-metre aluminium ladder through the desert, dusted the earth drawings with chalk and thus enabled the first close-up photos to be taken. Finally she began to measure the figures and to copy them faithfully to scale.

[3]

[4]

Reiche soon realized that the scrape drawings were not distributed randomly through the landscape, but that they always appeared where 'several straight lines intersect'.[10] In addition she found that there was only *one* monkey, spider, whale, dog, etc, but more than 20 bird-figures. The prehistoric people who had carved these creatures into the earth must have had a preference for birds. And another thing: in the whole *flat* region, no single human figure was to be found, nor any human face, although there *were* a number of these on the sheer cliff-walls of the Palpa region, near Nazca. Here were depicted human heads from which rays streamed out, others with antennae-like headgear, and a 29-metre-high figure pointing to the sky with its right arm, to the earth with its left. A picture riddle from the past. Also remarkable, and crying out to be deciphered, were the many geometrical patterns – often, though not always, linked to the drawings of animals. From the network of trails, a 1.5-kilometre, ruler-straight line shoots out, and connects with the 60-metre-high giant monkey. Beneath the feet of this animal lie seven great prongs. Each foot has three toes, one hand has four fingers and the other five.[3] From the tail of the monkey the straight line carries on into a geometrical pattern, consisting of 16 zigzag lines of equal length. Higher mathematics?

There are more such mathematical conundrums, and perhaps my pictures will inspire a maths freak to try to work out a solution.

A particularly hard nut to crack is the 'double labyrinth'. Three narrow, absolutely straight, parallel lines appear from nowhere. Each ends in a right angle in a broader 'paper-clip'. Five of these 'paper-clips' stand in a row next to one another like a rank of soldiers, and are connected to one another at their base.[4] From the last 'paper-clip' a narrower line branches off and ends in the 'double labyrinth'. This consists of two neighbouring, right-angular labyrinth forms, whose lines allow passage both from the outside in and from the inside out. But this is not all. Putting a sharp pencil to these forms and tracing their paths, one finds on the other side of them a further six 'paper-clips', the last of which is once more connected to a narrow line, many kilometres in length, which disappears somewhere on the horizon. To sum up, there are five 'paper-clips' next to each other, then two

[5]

connected labyrinths, and finally six 'paper-clips'. As a child I often drew patterns without taking my pencil off the paper. This pattern is the same kind of thing.

On the spirit road

So most of these remarkable patterns were not simply placed into the landscape in isolation – they are also connected with each other, sometimes over great distances. On the Pampa de Jumana, for instance, immediately after the second bend in the road leading from the Ingenio valley to the pampa plateau, one finds a huge network of broad trails and narrow lines. From the trails and trapezoidal-shaped surfaces on the ground, narrow lines lead off into infinity. The longest line so far discovered is no less than 23 kilometres long.[5] Crazy!

A threefold line south of Palpa is particularly intriguing, a riddle begging to be solved. At first glance one might think there are only two lines, which begin somewhere or other and run parallel, at a

[6]

distance of 2 metres from each other, like wheel tracks. But on closer observation this turns out to be an optical illusion: only the right-hand trail consists of *one* line, while the left-hand one is formed of *two* lines separated by only a hair's breadth. The distance between them is about 10 centimetres. A wheel-track with three wheels? Hardly, for the three lines run straight as the crow flies over crevices and clefts towards the summit of the next hill, about 2.5 kilometres away. And what do we find on the top of the hill, where the lines end? Nothing. At least, nothing as far as we can tell, in the absence of any experimental drilling, let alone chemical analysis of the soil. But I'll come back to that later.

And there are other parts of this enormous joke of a plateau that might also be well served by some deep drilling: for instance, at the point where two 50-metre-wide runways meet at an oblique angle, with narrower lines converging from all sides.[6] I counted 21 of them. So what is at the centre? At another place countless narrow lines radiate from all possible directions towards the end of a trail, like a

[7]

[8]

crown of rays. But these are not small, 5-metre-long 'rays'; they are hundreds of metres long, some even several kilometres long. Is there something important to be found at the point where all these paths meet? Could one discover something there by using certain measuring processes? Is there a riddle to be solved here?

Even hikers or tourists without the money for a flight over the plateau can see such a 'ray-hill'. There is one right next to the road, almost exactly 22 kilometres outside the little town of Nazca. Walking over the Nazca plain is strictly forbidden, but this rule does not apply to the small elevation on the right side of the road. Its summit is 512 metres above sea-level, but it is only 34 metres higher than the road. In spite of this tiny difference in height, it is worth climbing.[7, 8] Looking northwards across the road you can see two lines next to each other, and 20 metres further on another pair of lines. Both pairs of lines run towards the hill you're standing on. In the other direction the right-hand parallel lines end in a single trail after 3 kilometres, while the left-hand lines run for 2.5 kilometres before just touching the so-called 'dragon fly' drawing, then they too end in a trail, 1.3 kilometres long. To see these runways, though, you will need binoculars or a zoom lens, for at 34 metres you are not high enough to have a clear view. But these two pairs of lines are not the only ones which converge on this small hill. From almost all directions single lines appear from nowhere, and end beneath your feet. So what does this hill conceal? What is special about its position? Has anyone ever drilled here to find out, or has a magnetic field measurement ever been taken?

No need for that, say the self-elected Nazca-experts, very few of whom have ever spent more than 48 hours in the region – if they were ever there at all! The mysteries of Nazca have long since been cleared up, they say. Have they? I would like to demonstrate that we know virtually nothing; and the little we think we know is based on false assumptions, wrongly interpreted data and a whole series of prejudices.

There are a good many lines which run towards hills, cross and intersect on them, or end abruptly. The whole crazy web of these lines seems endless. For me, the most incomprehensible is the 62-metre-wide trail which ascends a small hill then spreads out from the summit

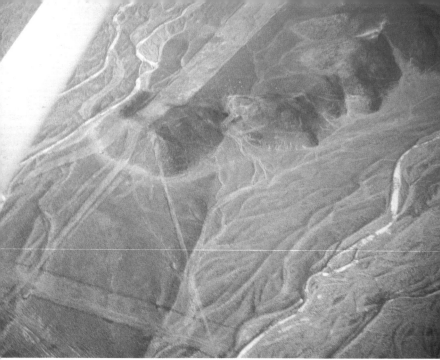

[9]

in several narrower lines. It looks like a ski-jump which five imaginary skiers ascend together, then take off from in different directions at the highest point.[9] The middle of these five narrower lines carries on for 10 kilometres through the plain.

There is no end to the shapes, runways and lines. One starts to feel entangled in a strange spirit road of hallucinations. To keep some kind of clarity in all the confusion, it's important to differentiate between four kinds of marking:

1 Runways: the word 'runway' doesn't have to mean 'airstrip', although one can't help being reminded of one. This category of marking also includes the broad tracks which lead towards the runways. In Spanish, the same word is used – the local inhabitants and the pilots refer to them both as 'las pistas'.

2 Narrow lines: about a metre wide, usually connected to the runways, and often several kilometres long. There are more than 2,000 of these narrow lines!

14

3 Geometrical figures: zigzag lines, 'paper-clips', spirals or strange patterns. They are sometimes linked to the animal drawings – for example the monkey – and sometimes pass either over or under the runways.

4 Scrape drawings: representations of an iguana, whale, dog, monkey, spider, flower, birds, etc. So far 32 of these scrape drawings have been discovered. They are so called because it is assumed they were scraped out of the ground.

Images without instruments?

Available research and popular literature on the subject can easily lead one to believe that these scrape drawings are the be-all and end-all of the extraordinary plain of Nazca. Any tourist who gets flown over the plateau for half an hour will come away with the same false impression.

But, as Maria Reiche pointed out, 'the animal figures are only tiny, isolated forms, scattered here and there between gigantic geometrical drawings'.[11] The well-documented scrape drawings are, at most, a small fraction of Nazca's riddle, minute in comparison to the runways, trapezoids and narrow lines. The fish is just 25 metres in size, the spider 46, the monkey about 60 metres and the condor 110. The biggest, the humming bird with its long beak, measures 250 metres.[10]

Though they are on a far smaller scale than the runways and lines, the question remains: How were they made? Maria Reiche points out that all their proportions are in perfect harmony. As a trained geographer and mathematician who put great emphasis on exact measurement, she observed:

> The originators of these drawings, who would only have been able to view the perfection of their creations from the air, must have first planned and drawn them to a small scale. How they subsequently enlarged these drawings, giving each line its right place and proportions, is a riddle that will take years to solve. Only someone who knows the techniques a surveyor employs can fully appreciate the sort of skill which would have been required to transpose a small-scale drawing onto a giant area, and retain complete accuracy of proportion. The Peruvians must have possessed instruments and tools of which we know nothing, and which, alongside other secret knowledge, they concealed from the eyes of their conquerors ...[12]

What kinds of 'instruments and tools'? Who were these teachers or priests of genius who demonstrated to the simple Indian peoples their geometrical arts? And what was the purpose of it all? No one does anything without a reason, least of all when such long periods of time are involved – which I will later show to be the case. We don't know what 'instruments and tools' were applied in constructing the intricate animal forms. It has been suggested that stakes were used, to which were tied cords of varying lengths. This would allow circles to be constructed. Yet the animal drawings rarely consist of regular half- or quarter-circles. The monkey's curling tail might have been formed by means of the simple 'stake-cord' method, but such a method would not have been of any use for the dog, humming bird, whale and other so far unidentified fabulous creatures.

The straight lines on the other hand could very easily have been staked out with cords. But what was the point of the zigzag lines, 'paper-clips', spirals, labyrinths and other seemingly senseless geometric patterns?

One of these curious forms consists of six main lines which together measure roughly 600 metres in length. As in the labyrinth, the end of each line is connected to its neighbouring line. Within this network of lines there is also a long arrow of 400 metres, culminating in a point. The arrow is likewise joined to a neighbouring line and a nearby square. If you were to walk the entire length of this geometrical form (roughly 5 kilometres), it would take you a good hour. If, on the other hand, you just walked straight across it, four minutes would be enough. At first sight it may seem pointless to take an hour when four minutes will get you to the same place. So was it a kind of processional path? But, if so, where are the signs of foot- or sandal-prints? At the edge of this long-drawn-out geometrical curiosity there are three small scrape drawings: a kind of lizard; something that looks like a poorly-drawn tree (or, according to Reiche, seaweed); and a vague sort of body from which sprout two hands (or feet?), one with five fingers, the other with four.

Whatever made the earth engravers draw these images? What was the common factor in all of them? If the animal figures are 'perfect and harmonious in their proportions' (Reiche), why does the little monster next to the geometrical form have five fingers on one hand and four on the other? Why does the monkey have three toes, and four fingers on one hand and five on the other?

Close to the place where the plain suddenly slopes down into the Ingenio valley lies a spiral of six circles with an 'S'-turn in the middle. The outermost circle is 80 metres in diameter. Passing straight through the spiral to its centre runs a path that starts 50 metres below in the valley.[11] The spirals and path must have been made *before* the geophysical processes occurred which brought about the subsidence of the land at this point. In the other direction, the spiral lies at the end of a runway 53 metres wide and 700 long. At 80 metres to the left of this is another runway, 70 metres wide and 720 metres long. This runway intersects at right angles with a 'main runway' that is a

[11]

[12]

kilometre long and 95 metres broad. Crazy? But there's still more. To the right of the runway which ends in the spiral is a small slipway (18 metres wide, 360 metres long). And at the end of that lies a labyrinth form. So what's going on?

Under and over

Under all these runways spreads a baffling network of geometrical forms. I emphasize the word under because it can be shown that the geometrical forms were drawn *first*, and the runways laid down later on.[12] It will come as no surprise that many of the narrow, ruler-straight, kilometre-long lines also run towards these runways.

Unfortunately there are only very limited and imperfect maps of the Nazca region. The best of them – on a scale of 1:10,000, published by the Instituto Geografica Nacional – shows an impressive section of the Ingenio valley and the Pampa de Jumana. On it, many runways, straight lines and scrape drawings are reproduced to scale and in the

[13]

[14]

correct north–south orientation. Yet this map covers only roughly a quarter of the patterns to be found there. In the autumn of 1995 I was able, from an aeroplane, to take 1,000 excellent photographs. I have not found their equivalent among the available maps. Of course there are land and road maps, but they tell us nothing about the riddle of Nazca. I enquired further of the Peruvian airforce, and the pilots who fly tourists over the plateau. But there simply are no maps that show the earth markings in any proper detail. 'How could there be?' laughed the chief pilot Eduardo. 'Hardly a day goes by when we don't make some new discovery!'

From the aeroplane – from which the door had been removed – I was able to photograph two controversial sections of marking:

1 A clearly recognizable runway, about 70 metres broad and 800 metres long. At the edge of a cliff to the right of the runway a spiral, and then, carved like a tattoo on skin, a broad zigzag pattern. This zigzag pattern runs – in such a pronounced way that blind people would be able to make it out – *under* the runway.[13, 14] The conclusion

[15]

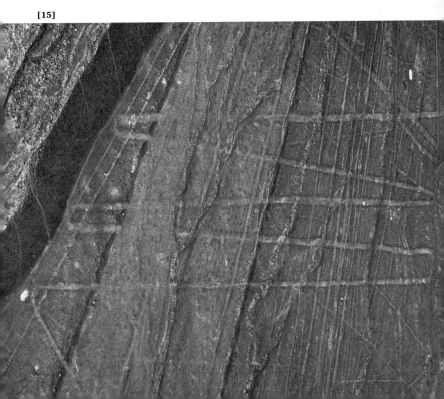

cannot be avoided that the geometrical pattern was carved first and the runway laid over it at a later date.

2 The second photograph shows the exact opposite: a clearly recognizable runway *over* which a zigzag pattern runs.[15] These zigzags are closer together than in the first picture. Was the runway there first and then covered with the zigzag pattern? I am not sure – it almost seems as if these zigzags too were originally *under* the runway, and as a result of thousands of years of erosion have risen to the surface. I am more and more perplexed about the significance of these zigzags. What was the purpose of such ornamentation if it was later to have a broad highway flung down over it, that hid two-thirds of it from view? Or is it nothing to do with ornament? Are the zigzag lines connected with some long-forgotten technology, such as what we nowadays call 'induction-control loops'?

This is a heretical question: it opens a wound that we're supposed to leave well alone. Yet the pictures speak for themselves. The broad zigzag lines *under* the runway are, at the end of the day, only one part of the conundrum. Four narrow lines run along the runway's left-hand side, and beside them lies a spiral formed from five concentric circles. To the right of it pass six thin, straight lines, which then vanish *under* the runway. Why would anyone ever need broad zigzags and filament-fine strips passing *underneath* a trail? Were they a way of marking something? Some kind of script? Some kind of message? Of what use would they have been once a runway had been laid over them?

Neither ornament nor message then, but just a quirk of history? Did some ancient generation – to whom it had not yet occurred to draw runway-like trails in the desert – start off by making geometrical drawings, with no inkling perhaps that later generations would come along and cover up their handiwork with highways? But this in turn presupposes that the later 'runway builders' thought nothing of the drawings of their forefathers. Hardly a very satisfactory theory. There was after all plenty of space to lay down runways elsewhere. Why did they have to be plonked down directly on top of the geometrical patterns? What was so important about this particular position?

But there is another reason why this kind of logic doesn't get us very far: there are also runways *over* other runways!

Proof of this is an aerial photograph I took – not of the level ground of the desert plateau, but of a flattened hilltop in the region of Palpa.[16] Both runways begin almost at the same point, but diverge at an angle of 45 degrees. In a way similar to flight-orientation markings on the approach to an airport, there are nine narrow lines before the runway proper begins. (I have not included the central, brighter line, as I suspect that this was made in modern times by some kind of vehicle.) *Underneath* the right-hand runway, an older, much broader and larger one can clearly be seen. I estimate this underlying runway to be 80 metres wide and 1.3 kilometres long. So a runway of smaller dimensions has been laid on top of an older and larger one.

A further photograph shows the same runways from another perspective.[17] This allows us a clear view of the whole business: the new runway, and below it the older and broader one. *Over* the older runway runs a shorter geometrical pattern. But this still remains *underneath* the newer runway. So, as far as can be judged by what's in front of us, we have the sequence: old runway/geometrical pattern/ new runway. We can safely conclude from this that the 'runway-building age' must have lasted for a considerable period. How long? Archaeological research tells of a culture that was active from roughly AD 500 onwards. This date is based on a wooden stake that was found in the middle of a pile of stones. Carbon-dating analyses ascertained it to be from AD 525 (with a possible error variation of 80 years). I would personally not attach too much importance to this. The fact that someone placed a wooden stake in a pile of stones in the 6th century does not mean that the runways hadn't already existed for a very long time.

How old did you say?

Maria Reiche testified that the whole thing must have carried on for 'hundreds of years'.[13] Peruvian authors even say that the oldest runway dates back 4,000 years.[14] Nobody knows the truth. The few scientific datings that have been undertaken are all contradictory and questionable. Who can guarantee that some little fire, from whose remains carbon datings are made, is not much younger than the runways and markings? There ought to be countless fire-sites, left by all the different generations of people who at some time worked in the pampa, carrying away stones and laying out marking ropes. There ought to be remains of food and small pieces of clothing. But there is nothing. It is as if the pampa Indians had dissolved into thin air. Nowhere has there been found an imposing monument that might have been erected in memory of the chief priest or the chief surveyor. No holy place or temple to commemorate princes or priests. No inscription to give any clues about the legendary race which immortalized itself on the Nazca plain. Unless of course the drawings and lines themselves are such an inscription.

How many stones must have been carried away altogether? Just think: there are more than 2,000 narrow lines, some of which are 3, 5, 6, 10, even more than 20 kilometres long. Interspersed with these are trapezoid surfaces, up to 80 metres at their broadest point, converging to a narrow line after 3.6 kilometres. Then there are the runways, from 30 to 110 metres wide and up to 1.4 kilometres long. And finally the scrape drawings, consisting of roughly 100 spirals and geometrical figures. And the runways which are laid *over* other runways.

Reading the literature about Nazca one gets the impression that the whole thing was childishly easy – that the Indians needed to do nothing more than clear the desert surface of the smaller stones to reveal the lighter-coloured undersurface. 'Placing one's foot down is enough to reveal the lighter ground beneath, and to leave a lasting trace.'[15] This is not true, nor is it sufficient explanation. The ground of the diverse pampas around Nazca is composed of alluvial deposits, interspersed with flint, slate, chalk and volcanic rock. The surface stones have been exposed for thousands of decades to extreme variations of temperature. On winter nights, the temperature sinks to 4 degrees Celsius, while the daytime temperature rises to 40 degrees. Heat and cold crumble the stones to gravel, similar to the kind laid down between railway sleepers. The heat also oxidizes the surface stone, so that it assumes a rust-brown colour. As it crumbles, dust is released, some of which settles on the ground, some of which is blown away on the wind.

[18]

[19]

[20]

26

This geological process leaves the undersurface undisturbed. If the rust-brown stones are cleared away, a lighter-coloured layer is revealed. This is how the scrape drawings were made – I have tried it myself at several places. Sometimes it works, sometimes it doesn't. The desert surface is often so hard that 'kicking away' the stones with one's shoes achieves nothing – no lighter colour appears. On the other hand, there is no doubt that the cars and motorbikes which have been driven over the pampa since the fifties have left behind livid tracks. These ugly scars often destroyed and cut across the ancient ground markings. But in spite of this clear fact, something still puzzles me.

Today the undersurface revealed by the figures, runways and lines is hardly any brighter than the rest of the surface. Everything looks fairly uniform – except perhaps for the figures which Maria Reiche and others dusted with chalk or swept with brooms. It is therefore all the more astonishing that the giant signs and tracks on the surface of the desert can be so clearly distinguished from an aeroplane. Why is this so? Any tourist 'doing' Nazca can climb the metal observation tower next to the road and see five lines and the outline of a runway from this vantage point. Yet there is no colour difference between the lines and the rest of the surface, no lighter undersurface to be seen. On each of my visits to Nazca I also took photographs at ground level. Only very rarely did the lines and trails show any colour difference. So I am forced to ask: What's going on here? How is it that we can see these figures at all – let alone so clearly – when nowadays everything consists of the same, uniform rust-brown colour? [18, 19] Why is it that not only the contours but also the entire surface of the runways appear as a distinct yellow-white in contrast to the rest of the pampa, as though they had once been covered in plaster, although at ground level they seem the same colour as their surroundings? Why, for heaven's sake, can the roughly 1-metre-wide zigzag lines be so clearly differentiated from the runways – even when they lie *beneath* them? Was another kind of material used? Apart from being ground cleared of surface stones, did the runways and lines originally consist of something else? All nonsense? Pure, unfounded speculation? Let me present some solid evidence.

No one can dispute that a zigzag line runs *under* the runway shown in photograph 13. If, as has been claimed, the trail-makers just scraped away little stones from the surface to reveal the lighter undersurface, then the zigzag lines would also have vanished. To reveal the lighter chalk colour of the undersurface, *all* stones have to be cleared away. The zigzag pattern would therefore have been cleared away as well unless it was composed of some other, additional, material. And did this zigzag perhaps have a quite different purpose from the one attributed to it by archaeologists stubbornly pursuing the 'religious ritual' train of thought?

Leaving these questions aside, the creators of the message of Nazca must certainly have cleared away an enormous amount of stones – for the depressions in the desert surface in which the lines and runways lie are up to 30 centimetres deep to this day. One can still frequently observe piles of stones on either side of the trails.[20]

But if all this toil and sweat on the desert and the surrounding hills and mountains began around AD 500 and continued for centuries – as work of such huge dimensions must have done – it would have gone on until the beginning of the Inca age, around the 13th century. So why didn't the Incas carry on the rituals and worship of their fore-fathers, if that's what it was? Why did all this scraping business stop? Why was this great performance, this mysterious 'runway' cult carried out only in the region of Nazca and to the north of it? It is true that many giant scrape drawings on cliffs and slopes can be found in the coastal region of Paracas (in Peru) and down as far as Antofagasta (in Chile), but runways and lines several kilometres long appear only in Nazca. Maria Reiche says:

> The creators of these lines chose this region in the knowledge that their works would be obliterated neither by wind nor rain: the wind just blows away any dust and sand that might cover up the trails; and before air pollution arrived, there was hardly any rain to speak of.[16]

There is no rain today either – apart from the ten minutes of drizzle per year. But if the ground scrapers chose this region 'in the knowledge' that nothing would vanish for a very long time, why did their successors not honour this intention, but instead scrape runways *over* the zigzag lines and earth markings? This cult, of whatever kind it was, must after all have been equally significant to later generations, for they would not otherwise have laid 'runways over runways'. And if this scratching and scraping continued for hundreds of years, as it clearly must have done, and – measured from the year 500 – went on until shortly before the beginning of the classical Inca period, around 1,200, why did no Inca ever say anything about it? Why did none of the Spanish chroniclers spare a single word for the curious markings around Nazca? Why did none of the Spanish soldiers, priests or traders notice this gigantic picture book in the Nazca desert?

My suspicion is that this is because the earth drawings are far older than has been assumed. When the Spanish conquistadores arrived, the Indians had long since forgotten the religion of the 'runway makers'. Their concerns revolved around the 'Sons of the Sun', their temples, fortifications, holy days, wars, and growing their daily bread. Giant markings in the ground? No one either knew or cared about such things.

Nazca archaeology is carried on in a much too superficial way – in all senses of the word. The answer such 'professionals' furnish us with is not sufficient to allay our hunger for the truth. They limit themselves to the usual half-baked ideas, instead of looking deeper. Anyone who tries to find out more, who applies more sharply honed thinking – even if only by asking awkward questions – is 'rocking the boat'. The magic word 'cult' is supposed to cover everything and solve all questions once and for all. Yet I haven't stopped asking questions, for the answers I have so far received are quite frankly unsatisfactory.

A catalogue of senseless questions

What did the creators of the lines and runways want to achieve? The calendar solution has long since proved redundant, and the possible connections between scrape drawings and astronomical constellations, even if true, cannot explain the runways. From where did the scrapers derive their geometrical knowledge? What instruments did they employ? Which 'measuring priests' decided upon the locations and proportions, and why? Onto what kind of maps did they transfer their calculations, on what kind of material did they draw the plans which were later to be enlarged to the huge dimensions of the scrape drawings? How was the work organized? Was work carried out at several places at once or only at one site? Was the marking carried out simply by clearing small stones away from the desert surface or was some additional material employed? Some kind of colour? Crumbled pieces of shining mica? Limestone dissolved in water? Why do zigzag lines and other patterns not vanish underneath the runways if the sole method of making these markings was by clearing stones?

How important were the specific proportions of the runways and trapezoid surfaces? What purpose did the lines serve, those that run for up to 20 kilometres and sometimes line up directly with a runway? What was the point of those lines which end suddenly at the summit of a hill or mountain and then diverge like a ski-jump?

Was there a particular overall plan? Was there an initial planning phase, or did each group of workers just get on with it however they pleased? Who organized the whole thing and orchestrated the armies of workers? How were they provided with water in the burning heat of the desert? If a team of scrapers worked for several months on a trapezoid surface of about 3 kilometres in length, they must have left their work-place each evening and returned every morning. So where are any signs of their foot-, sandal- or shoe-prints? There are only very few places where walking trails can be discerned, and they are all to be found in the mountains, close to the traces of old habitations. There are enormous runways in isolated spots in the middle of the plateau, without any trace of a path leading to them. If it is indeed true that the lighter undersurface of the desert was immediately revealed when anyone disturbed a pebble that had lain there for millennia, then countless footpaths ought to be visible. Several hundred people who march out to work then march back again in the evening can hardly fail to disturb the stones beneath their feet. So what happened to their traces? Nothing can be seen of them. Motorbikes and cars have left their ugly marks everywhere on the desert ground in a signature of yellowish-white lines. So where, even if they didn't use carts or chariots, are the footprints of the scrapers? They must have had feet, mustn't they?

Does some secret or mystery lie beneath the hills towards which many diverse lines radiate? What is concealed at the points in the broad plain where kilometre-long lines converge from all sides?[21]

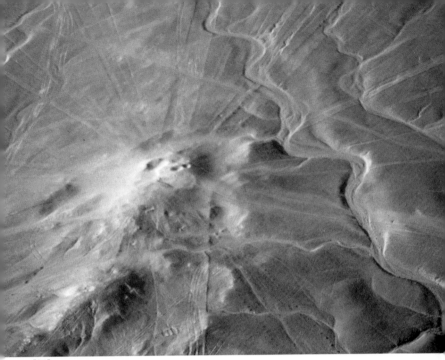

[21]

Why are no scientific measurements undertaken with modern instruments? Why does no one scrape away the surface of a runway to get through to the zigzag line below? Why does no one subject the material of the markings to chemical analysis?

A long long time ago, according to the official view, isolated water courses ran through the pampa. These can also be clearly seen from the aerial photographs. Why did these waters never flow *over* the trapezoid surfaces and runways of up to 3.6 kilometres in length?[22–26] Whoever suggests that the streams were there *before* the ground markings, and that the ground scrapers later laid their markings between them, is barking up the wrong tree. Although the water never covered the really long runways, there are many places where it did touch and encroach on them. This means that the ground markings must have been there *before* the water. Thanks to modern dating methods, it would be easy to find out which of the runways was the oldest, the 'ur'-runway as it were. Samples taken from a variety of runways would allow such analysis to be carried out – so why is no one

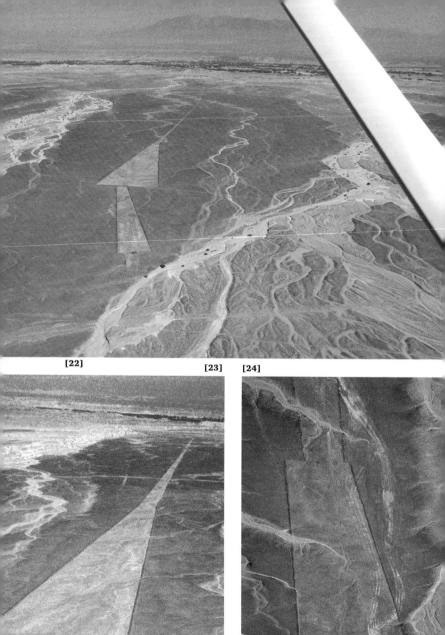

[22]   [23]   [24]

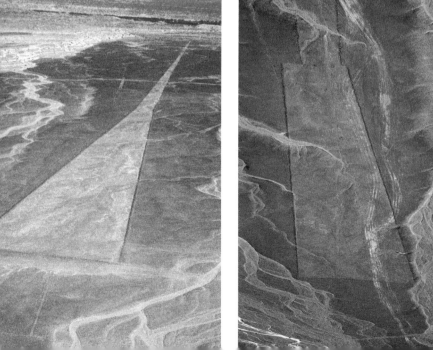

[25]

runways would allow such analysis to be carried out – so why is no one interested in doing this?

And what drove these ancient people to carry out all this work? What kind of cult or worship was it that spurred them on, for generation after generation, to such intensity of effort?

Some readers might object at this point and ask why Erich von Däniken doesn't supply some of the answers to these questions himself. Why doesn't *he* scrape away at a runway to reach the zigzag underneath? Why doesn't *he* organize the chemical analyses that he recommends? I would love to – if only I were allowed to!

After all sorts of mindless people had, in the sixties and seventies, wrecked parts of the drawings with their cars and motorbikes, the government of Peru finally intervened – and not a moment too soon. On the urgent recommendation of Maria Reiche the pampa of Nazca was officially declared an 'archaeological park'. Large roadsigns[27] announce this fact on all approaches to the region: no one is permitted to walk or drive over the pampa. Anyone ignoring this rule can be fined

33

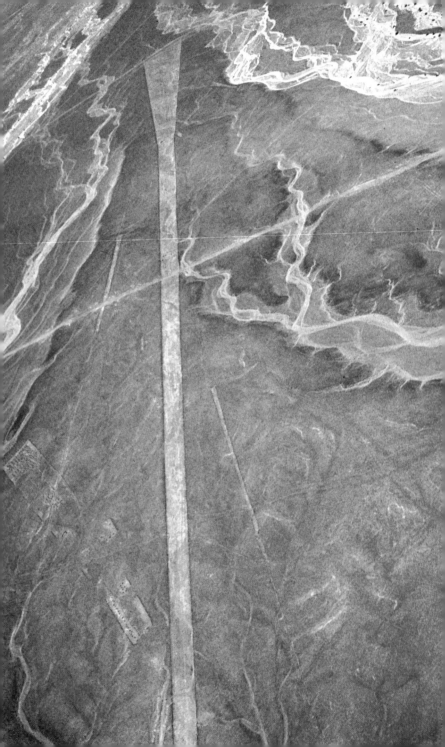

1 million US dollars and faces up to five years in prison. I can think of better ways of spending my time than languishing in a Peruvian lockup! And trespassing secretly has certain practical difficulties: the region is enormous and some kind of vehicle is essential to get to the various sites. And in those wide open spaces even a lonely hiker would soon be spotted by one of the small aircraft which daily fly tourists over the scrape drawings. The pilots have been told to radio back immediate news of any vehicle, group or individual seen below. Guards are posted at strategic points, such as the viewing tower I mentioned, and once notified immediately rush off on motorbikes to seize any trespassers.

But what about getting official permission? The Peruvian Cultural Institute in Lima is the place to turn for this. This has various sub-departments and also a Nazca protection office. The good thing about this is that Nazca gets the protection it needs. The bad thing is that a request may take years to process, the applicant must answer an endless catalogue of questions, and must of course subscribe to the prevailing opinions about Nazca without showing any desire to ask awkward questions. One starts to wonder if it is worth carrying out any research if it has to conform with certain strict provisos. The official view must always appear 'reasonable' and unimaginative, taking its point of departure from current ways of thinking and received opinion

[27]

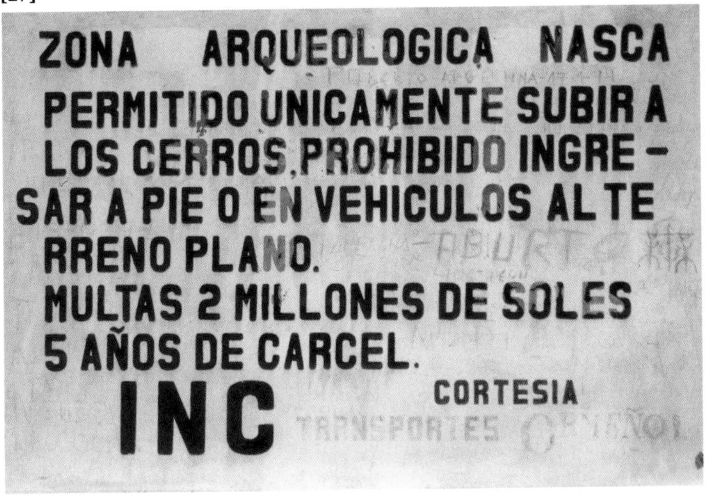

[26]

and theory. An example of this is the theory of the American archaeologist Helaine Silverman, who is apparently an 'Assistant Professor' of Anthropology.[17] She believes that 2,000 years ago a number of family clans gathered in the Nazca region to control the trade routes. Each clan appropriated a particular geometrical figure as a 'coat of arms'. To stake out and mark each piece of territory, these images were scraped out on a huge scale on the surface of the desert.

Voilà! The riddle of Nazca is solved and the scientific press disseminates this discovery as truth incarnate! There is nothing to be said against the idea of a possible family coat of arms, but the 'trade routes' and 'staked-out territories' theories don't hold water for a minute. Staking out territory in the arid desert regions of Nazca? Anyway, the 'coats of arms' often lie close to each other, are incomplete and could not possibly indicate territorial boundaries. No blade of grass, tree or bush grew there, there was nothing to harvest and therefore nothing to eat. OK, I know there are clever Dicks who will say it was different 2,000 years ago. Really? But *if* the pampa had enjoyed a different climate in those days, *if* it had been covered in a lush green, it would have been impossible to scrape away stones from the dry(!) surface to reveal the lighter layer beneath. You can't have it both ways. The 'coats of arms', in fact, tell us nothing about the runways. And to crown it all, how could the Indian clans have made anything of their 'family coats of arms', since they can be recognized only from the air?

So is it impossible to gather scientifically accurate information about the secrets of Nazca, and subject it to a cross-disciplinary analysis? What role was played by Maria Reiche, the grand old lady of Nazca?

And after Reiche?

All the honours possible in Peru were showered upon Maria Reiche. There are Maria Reiche schools, Maria Reiche streets,[28] a Maria Reiche Museum, a Maria Reiche Observation Tower. Even the airport at Nazca is named after her. Reiche became an honorary citizen of Peru and was decorated by President Alberto Fujimori with the nation's highest award, the Order of the Sun. The financial situation now is far better than it was in earlier decades, when Reiche had to pursue her

[28]

research alone and unsupported. Today there is at least one charitable foundation that would make funds available for solving the Nazca riddle. The work could begin immediately were it not for the hindrances continually being placed in its way by individuals and the government.

Doctor Maria Reiche herself is now over 90. Wind and sun have left their mark upon this great investigator. She has been blind and almost deaf for years. In earlier decades she held a lecture each evening for the guests of the Touristas Hotel in Nazca (now called the Lineas de Nazca). Then her sister Renate Reiche, a medical doctor, arrived from Stuttgart to support her. She also settled in Nazca and took over the nightly lectures from her ailing sister. Renate Reiche always became angry – and made no secret of it – when anyone dared to doubt the theories of her sister. In contrast to the more gracious Maria, Renate was a robust character who took most things in her stride. She died recently in Lima of a liver complaint.

Maria Reiche lives on, though her senses are rather befuddled by age. So I ask myself why so many interesting earth markings in the

Palpa region (north of Nazca, yet still part of the whole complex) do not appear in her *magnum opus* on the subject.[18] The answer is that only a part of this book, which appeared in 1993, was written by Maria Reiche. No less problematic for those who know her well was her decision to adopt a daughter – not a poor Peruvian child but a grown woman. This lucky person, who obviously found a way to Maria Reiche's heart, is called Anna Cogorno. I can't say exactly what went on, but I do know that Maria Reiche's money had something to do with it!

And meanwhile, in the Nazca plateau, nothing is happening. Those who have the desire and the means to get on with the work, have had their hands tied. The Reiche Foundation and the Nazca Protection Commission seem to have no interest in furthering research. Nor does the adopted daughter of Maria Reiche, who behaves as though the Reiche Foundation together with the whole plain of Nazca is her personal property. So what are serious-minded researchers supposed to do?

It is an undisputed fact that over a period of millennia different succeeding cultures inhabited the valleys around Nazca, especially the Ingenio valley. Archaeology tells us of 'Nazca 1 to Nazca 7'. The remains of around 500 settlements have been discovered, dating from 800 BC to AD 1,400. The Nazca region was therefore inhabited for a considerable period. The now irrigated Ingenio valley was once full of runways, narrow lines and trapezoid surfaces. The view from an aeroplane confirms this: on narrow strips at places on the surface which are lying fallow or are unirrigated, there are isolated but still just visible lines which run for 100 metres or so before being swallowed by green. This fact ought to astound us, but people fail to notice what's in front of their eyes. Just think about it: the fields are artificially irrigated and then cultivated with tractors and harrows. Then, a few years later, when certain fields are not irrigated or cultivated for some reason, when they are left fallow and dry out once more – hey presto, the lines suddenly start to reappear! This absolutely contradicts the official view that such markings were formed by just scraping away the gravel from the desert surface to reveal a lighter surface beneath. At various places in the Ingenio valley one can still find a variety of parallel lines and labyrinth patterns,[29] but probably not for much [29

longer: tractors have already 'cleaned up' a good deal of it, and are continuing their 'good work' at a steady rate.

Clay pots used by ancient peoples can be dated. So why should it not be possible to use similar methods to discover when the runways were created?

New datings

Archaeologists at the University of Illinois in Urbana, USA, *have* in fact dated the runways. Someone suggested that the runway builders must have had vessels to drink from, and that the remains of such vessels, which had occasionally fallen to the ground and broken, were likely to be found. So off they went to look, and found what they were looking for without much trouble – fragments of pottery here and there between the stones. Then began a great dating process with over a hundred samples – an arduous, long-winded process. If a number of pieces of pottery dating from 'Nazca 1' were found on a line or runway, logic would suggest that it had been made at that time. Unfortunately, bits of pottery from a range of *different* dates were often found close together. So what did that mean? Had inhabitants of 'Nazca 4' stumbled over old markings and dropped their vessels? Or did 'Nazca 5' people perhaps still own pots from a previous age, which had broken as they made their way through the desert? The whole picture started to seem very confused. On the other hand, roughly a quarter of the lines and runways could not be dated at all using these methods, 'because no pieces of ceramic were found', or because 'the fragments of pottery were so eroded that no satisfactory dating could be made'.[19]

I'm afraid that all this energetic dating work doesn't, in my view, seem to prove much. The oldest runways may have existed for a very long time before others came and renewed them. Nazca was no doubt some kind of holy place, a place of pilgrimage. It was immense and unique. So over the centuries, people must continually have come to visit it – and since it was very hot, would have brought with them clay vessels to drink from. Perhaps tired pilgrims chucked away their empties, as happens in tourist spots to this day. So now we discover such remains and conclude from them something about the age of the original trails. As far as I can see, the only safe conclusion one might draw would be that the greatest number of pottery remains would be found on the oldest markings – since over the years more people would have come to visit them. None of this explains, though, why there are lines as long as 23 kilometres, why three lines converge at the summit of a hill and then suddenly end, or why zigzag lines do not vanish although covered over by a runway.

Another annoying circumstance is that many archaeologists and amateur researchers focus exclusively on Nazca. The plain of Nazca actually represents not much more than an imitation of a much older 'runway culture', which originally stretched over the Palpa region. Compared with Palpa, the Nazca plateau is, apart from the scrape drawings and a few runway configurations, just a cheap copy. The desert surface of Nazca – which, by the way is far from flat (and we'll come back to this) – boasts quite a few low-quality runways, done 'on the cheap' by simply raking away the surface stones. These still line the edges of the runways and there is therefore no mystery about how they were made.

But in the Palpa region, about ten minutes' flight away from Nazca, the ground markings stare up at us in a mysterious, provoking kind of way, as though challenging us to solve their riddle. Although the Palpa region is also referred to as a plain, only the smallest part of it is actually flat. Palpa is in the mountains, and the runways lie upon artificially flattened hilltops, between which are several valleys. Extremely ingenious use has been made here of the natural lie of the land with its sudden sheer plunges. And just as in Nazca, there is no sign of the footprints of the human ant-armies which must have been working here.

One of the Palpa runways is flanked on both sides by double parallel lines. *Underneath* it there are clearly observable narrow lines, which run towards the runway at a steep angle. One end of these narrow lines connects in a short curve with one of the parallel lines. And as though to cap it all, the beginning of the runway boasts four step-like levels. The question of what came first – runway, narrow parallel lines or steps – is not relevant, for it must all have been created as part of one plan, in which all the elements are integral. The 'steps' belong as much to the runway as does the underlying line,

[30]

[31]

[32]

otherwise they wouldn't harmonize so elegantly with the right parallel line.[30, 31]

Who, in the light of such markings, can still justify the assertion that they were formed by simply 'carting away' small stones, or that they represent nothing more than the 'coat of arms' of some Indian clan?

Only a few valleys further on, the 'scrape' theory becomes wholly absurd. The roughly 60-metre-wide, 700-metre-long runway extends over several mountain summits. To level the ground for the runway, the peaks had first to be flattened and the material carried away.[32] In other words, before anyone could lay down the runway with its *underlying* zigzags, initial 'pioneer' work was needed to prepare the surface. Scraping away stones would not have done the trick. It gradually becomes clear that much of what we read about Nazca can at best be only half the truth – or more likely half the untruth.

In the region around Nazca there are mountains which are level as tables – as though they had been planed by a giant.[33] Yet the 'normal' mountains of the region by no means share this appearance.[34]

[33]

[34]

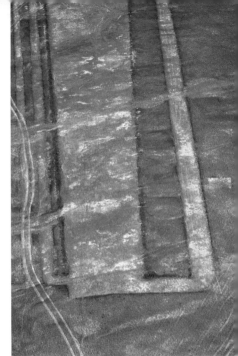

In the Ingenio valley, between the plain of Nazca and the mountains of Palpa, lie two runways of the most 'modern' design: from the end of one a kind of 'slipway' branches off and then runs parallel to the main runway.[35] The broad end of the other runway is flanked on both sides by 'slipways'.[36] Whether one likes it or not, the impression of a modern airstrip is undeniable. I cannot help asking myself what model the stone-age Indians were basing these designs on.

The wheel tracks on these photos are from cars and motorbikes of our own times. Some idiots obviously couldn't resist the temptation to roar about over the lines and runways. What is astonishing, though, is that there are again no signs whatsoever of the footprints of the runway makers. The argument that such footprints have been blown away by the wind over centuries (or millennia) is just so much hot air. If footprints had been blown away, why are the narrow lines next to the runway still visible? They are, after all, no wider than footpaths. The wind, as far as I am aware, does not act selectively, sparing the narrowest of lines while erasing footpaths. And whoever suggests

[37]

[38]

[39]

that the scrapers were careful to walk *inside* the lines and runways, would still, surely, have to admit that one footpath at least would, at some point, have to lead to the lines. The scrapers couldn't have just flown there.

The plain of Nazca, the partially cultivated Ingenio valley and the mountains of Palpa seem to thwart every theory thrown up to explain them. How can one explain a figure[37, 38] that has a regular pattern of holes on its surface? Nowadays these holes consist of small piles of stones, upon which the odd weed grows. They must once have had a function, for the runway starts with 11 holes, then, after a hole-free gap there follows a regular pattern of holes. So how do we crack this one?

Even more curious is the giant Y-runway.[39] The main runway, 90 metres broad, branches into two forks and then into some narrower lines which must be an integral part of the whole 'work' since they are connected to the Y in a geometrically precise way. Equally incomprehensible is a trapezoid surface that connects to an equal-sided

47

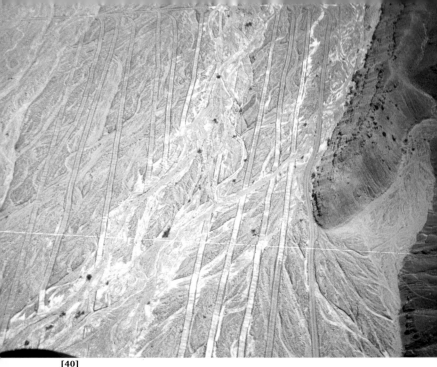

[40]

triangle.[22] From the peak of the triangle a narrow, bent line runs for about 2 kilometres into the distance. On both sides of this marking are signs of water, which floods the Nazca plain once in a blue moon. Strangely, the water has not encroached on the marking itself.

There are also peculiar strips which from the air remind one of some kind of 'gene map', however ridiculous such a comparison may seem. (Let me say quickly that they are certainly no such thing, in case anyone thinks of asserting that I believe the Nazca lines to be a 'gene-picture'.) The strips are subdivided by small black sections[40] and are 1.30 metres wide.

And finally there is the runway which the pilots nowadays refer to as the 'ET airport'. It begins as a broad surface and continues for 3.2 kilometres, gradually becoming narrower in the process. The pilots carry out 'pretend landings' over it: from a height of 1,000 metres they fly down towards the start of the runway, to a height of 3 metres, before ascending again. This is an incredible experience for the tourists – not unlike a Space Shuttle landing, perhaps.

48

There is much more to say about Nazca – things which are still more mysterious and incomprehensible, such as the geometrical key etched into the ground millennia ago by a wise mathematician. But before I speak of such things, I'd like to slip in an extra chapter which – who knows – might have a lot to do with the ancient engravers of Nazca.

Notes

1 Toribio Mejia Xesspe, *Acueductos y caminos antiguos de la hoya del Rio Grande de Nazca*, Actas y Trabajos Cientificos del XXVII Congreso 1939, vol. 1, Congreso International de Americanistas, Lima, pp. 559–69, 1940.

2 Paul Kosok, *The Mysterious Markings of Nazca,* Natural History, vol. 56, 1947.

3 Paul Kosok and Maria Reiche, *Ancient Drawings on the Desert of Peru,* Archaeology, vol. 2, 1949.

4 Maria Reiche, *Geheimnis der Wüste*, Stuttgart, nd.

5 Erich von Däniken, *Chariots of the Gods?*, London, 1968.

6 Félix Légare, 'Les lignes de Nazca, Trop belles pour être vraies', *La Revue Québec Science*, 1995.

7 Erich von Däniken, *Zurück zu den Sternen*, Dusseldorf, 1969.

8 Erich von Däniken, *Meine Welt in Bildern*, Dusseldorf, 1973.

9 Erich von Däniken, *Habe ich mich geirrt?*, Munich, 1985.

10 Reiche, op. cit.

11 Kosok and Reiche, op. cit.

12 Reiche, op. cit.

13 Ibid.

14 Marcela Gomez, 'El Misterio de la Pampa', *Aboard*, Aero Peru, February 1992.

15 Hermann Kern et al. on Maria Reiche, *Peruanische Erdzeichen*, Munich, 1974.

16 Ibid.

17 Helaine Silverman, 'Beyond the Pampa: The Geoglyphs in the Valleys of Nazca', *National Geographic Research and Exploration*, 1990, pp. 435–56.

18 Maria Reiche, *Contributiones a la Geometrie y Astronomia en el antiguo Peru*, Lima, 1993.

19 Silverman, op. cit.

2

A MAFIA OF FORGERS?

You can't legislate against rumour.
JOHANN NESTROY, 1801–1862

....

Only 150 kilometres north of the little town of Nazca, lies the provincial capital Ica. There, in the middle of town, on the Plaza de Armas, lives the family of Dr Janvier Cabrera.[41] He is the owner of a curious collection of thousands of engraved stones, which I wrote about at length in my book *Beweise* (von Däniken's proof).[1] His collection contains old and new engravings, authentic and fake. I searched out one of the fakers and reported on his forging process, but I also found geological authentication for the truly ancient pieces, and had microscopic photographs taken which proved their age.

Since then, 20 years have passed. Whenever I was in Peru I visited Dr Cabrera, and over the years developed a warm friendship with him. Once, about 14 years ago, the Cabrera family acted as hosts to one of my tour groups. We were sampling the local drink, *pisco sour*, when Cabrera suddenly took me aside. He told me that he would like to show me something which only very few of his close friends had so far seen. In the inner courtyard of his house, he pulled a giant key from his pocket and opened a door which led into a long, dark room. He flicked on the light-switch and ushered me inside.

At first I was speechless. To the right and left of the narrow passage I saw sturdy wooden shelves reaching from the floor to the ceiling, and on them hundreds upon hundreds of figures, close together and in rows one behind the other.[42, 43]

[41]

[42]

[43]

[44]

'What are they?' I asked him.

'A collection of unfired clay figures, from a civilization which existed 20,000, or perhaps 50,000, or even 100,000, years ago.'

'And where do they come from?' I asked, astonished.

'From the depot,' he answered drily.

As my eyes gradually grew accustomed to the dim light, they first made out a figure roughly 80 centimetres high. It stood upon the floor and grinned up at me.[44] A round pair of eyes stared out of large eye-sockets, reminding me of an owl. Close beside it I noticed a second figure, holding some kind of animal to its breast.[45] I immediately made a connection to similar figures which I had seen in the archaeological park in San Augustin, in Colombia, though they had been far larger and of stone. Then, at eye-level, I saw a figure with two heads, one above the other.[46, 47] That was also familiar to me from San Augustin. As I reached to pick up a toad-like figure with an outsize neck, a large cockroach ran across the rack – and I saw that the place was full of these beasties.

[45] ▷

52

[46]   [47]

On the ground were boxes, many of them stacked on top of each other, crammed to bursting with the strangest figures, all wrapped in newspaper. A crazy menagerie.

'Look, Erich,' said Cabrera, interrupting the thoughts whirling round in my head. In his hands he was balancing a human figure with an ape-like expression. This figure held a telescope in both hands and stared upwards through it. Wow! I thought – for I had seen a very similar figure, complete with telescope, among the engraved stones.[48, 49] In his left hand Cabrera held out to me a pterosaur, on which rode a human being with the head of a bird. The stone collection also boasted several such figures. Before leaving the room I caught sight of something at eye-level on the racks that looked like a tennis racket made of clay. Yet this 'racket' was adorned with strange pictures. There were 12 such rackets lying one against the other.[50] Who, for heaven's sake, would forge such things?

When I returned to my tour group, one of Cabrera's daughters came and sat down by me – the productive Cabreras have a family of eight.

[48]

[49]   [50]

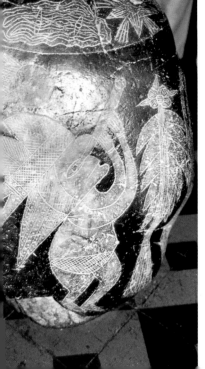

'Erich,' said the young lady, and looked at me seriously, 'please believe my father. What he says is true. The figures come from an underground depot and are incredibly old.' There were tears in her eyes, I saw, and I asked her why she was upset.

'The archaeologists of Peru won't take my father seriously. They *can't* take him seriously.'

'Why?'

'If they took him seriously they would also have to believe in his collection of stone and clay figures. They can't do that without blowing their archaeological opinions to smithereens. And if they thought my father's figures were real, they would all have to be confiscated. The government would soon find out what a precious treasure my father is sitting on. According to Peruvian law, archaeological finds cannot remain the property of a private individual – they belong to the state.'

All this was true, yet confused me still more. What was I supposed to think of this collection? Should I write about it and make myself a laughing stock? Should I expose Cabrera as a forger? If some Indian family had been working for him to produce these, why? Cabrera wasn't making a profit out of it, he wasn't selling them – on the contrary, he guarded them like a treasure under lock and key. He has never sold a single one.

Cabrera's daughter brought me back to the present.

'Erich, please write about this collection! Papa deserves it. You have no idea how he suffers. He is torn apart: the archaeologists and the government insist his figures cannot be real, yet he knows that they are!'

So I promised the girl to come back and examine this curious collection in more detail. Four years later I returned to Ica. But I had to postpone a lengthy examination – I wanted to do it properly, and such things can't be rushed. My plan was to at least partially empty the narrow room with the wooden racks, measure and compare the figures and take as many photos of them as possible. One criterion for the figures' authenticity would be their age. So during this visit I asked Dr Cabrera for some samples. He generously offered me the key. To be quite sure that I got a sample from a figure and not some other bit of clay from the ground, I broke the arm off a humanoid character and put it into a plastic bag. May Janvier Cabrera and all the ancient gods of Peru forgive me!

Who is Dr Cabrera?

So who is this Dr Cabrera and how did he come to possess his collection of engraved stones and clay figures?

The Cabreras are descended from an old family whose roots go back to the first generations of Spanish settlers. Janvier Cabrera was born in Ica on 13 May 1924. After completing his schooling he studied medicine in Lima, took his degree and subsequently worked for many years in the Hospital de Seguros Social in Ica. In 1961 Cabrera helped found the local university. In the meantime he had specialized in surgery and now became professor at the new university.

As a surgeon, Cabrera often operated on poor Indians who couldn't afford to pay for treatment. They rewarded him instead with dusty figures and engraved stones, which Cabrera himself originally believed to be forgeries. Until 1966, Cabrera had no interest whatsoever in archaeology.

Meanwhile, the brothers Carlos and Pablo Soldi, who ran a vineyard outside Ica and who had also been given engraved stones by the Indians, had begun to collect them. Cabrera knew the wine-growers and often laughed about their 'fake art collection'. The brothers had a different view. They believed the Indians. They made over the collection to the local museum, and soon specialists arrived from Lima to examine the stones. Although these experts carried out no scientific analyses, they pronounced the engravings to be modern forgeries, without exception. They said that the images on them were too manifold and contradictory, and did not fit in with current archaeological views. In spite of this, the engraved stones were put on show in the Ica museum (though were removed again in 1970).

On 13 May of the same year, Cabrera received as a birthday present from the photographer Felix Llosa Romero, a small stone engraved with a very curious motif. It was a kind of pterosaur, ridden by an Indian who controlled it with a staff.[51] Cabrera used the stone as a paperweight, but the more he looked at it, the more thoughtful he

[51]

became. Where did this motif come from? His schooling had of course taught him that no human being could ever have seen a dinosaur. All dinosaurs had died out about 60 million years ago, at a time when human beings did not exist.

At the next opportunity Cabrera asked Romero where his paperweight had come from. The latter advised him to drop such questions as it could be dangerous. There were, he said, tens of thousands of these engraved stones, and also thousands of clay figures. The 'simple' Indians were not so stupid. They guarded the legacy of their forefathers and knew that their collection of stones and clay figures would be decimated the moment its hiding place was known.

Cabrera, who was 42 at the time, didn't believe a word of this. But the same year, the Soldi brothers asked him if he'd like to buy some of their stones, for they had no room left to store them and would otherwise have to keep them in the open air. Cabrera went and had a look at their collection, shook his head and said that holding an exhibition of this 'modern art' might render the Indians a service.[52]

[52]

[53]

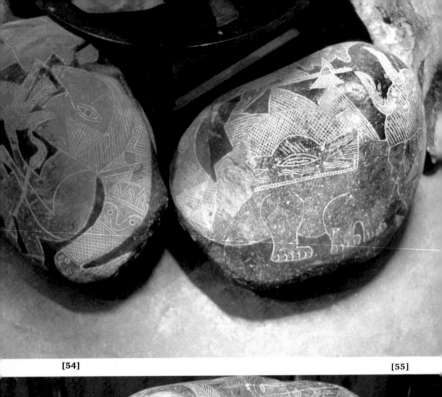

[54]   [55]

[56]   [57]

For the ridiculous sum of 7,000 old soles (worth about £30 in the currency of the time), Cabrera became the owner of 341 stones, which he deposited on an improvised rack in one of the rooms of his house.

The more he examined his collection in the coming months, the more astonished he became. There were many depictions of surgical operations – and that was something he knew about. But the practices illustrated on the stones were wholly at variance with his own knowledge of this subject. An engraving of a heart transplant – but where was the heart/lung machine necessary for it? Why no blood transfusion through the veins? What were the various tubes entering the patient's mouth?[53] Did the Indian forgers not know anything about modern surgery – were they just making it up out of their imagination? Where did they get the idea for the different dinosaurs on the engraved stones?[54, 55] And why were there images of Indians staring up at the starry sky through telescopes? Why, on some of the stones, were there maps and outlines of whole continents which simply didn't exist in reality?[56]

The stones gradually cast a spell over Cabrera. For the first time he began questioning the old farmers he had once treated, and who still came to him for advice. One man who was near death told him about a 'depot' where thousands of engraved stones and clay figurines were supposed to be stored. Cabrera remained sceptical, not least because obvious forgeries had in the meantime appeared and were being sold to tourists. The Indians weren't stupid. They knew ways of subsidising their pitiful wages. And the dying farmer had failed to reveal the exact spot where this secret depot was to be found. The more tourists visited Peru, the more etched stones were produced to sell to them. I visited one of these forgers, Basilo Uschuya, in 1973, and he openly admitted having forged all the stones, including those in Cabrera's collection.[57] This same forger – the one I had written about 20 years ago in proofs – had confided to a journalist named Andreas Fischer that the engraved stones were genuine, apart from the few hundred imitations he had made to sell to tourists. But, he said, he continued to pretend in public that they were all forged. Asked why, he replied: 'If I were to sell stones with genuine, ancient engravings, I'd get into big trouble with the local Indians – they take their cultural inheritance seriously. I'd also end up in prison.'

Cabrera, who was now far from sure what was meant by 'ancient' or 'modern', took four stones he thought must be genuine and had them analysed. The first certification was carried out by the geologist Dr Eric Wolf, from the mining company Mauricio Hochschild in Lima; the second by the Facultad de Minas of the Lima Technical College (under supervision of Dr Fernando de la Casa and Dr César Sotillo). Both confirmed the great age of the engraved stones. The analyses were based on the fact that the stones were covered in a fine, natural layer of oxidation that had to be many thousands of years old.[2] In 1976, together with the chief architect of NASA at that time, Joseph Blumrich, I visited Dr Cabrera. On that occasion he gave us four samples of ancient and new engravings. Under the microscope the difference between the false[58] and the genuine[59] engravings was indisputable.[3]

During the years, Cabrera had become more and more isolated. He had become confused about what was genuine and what was false, and unsettled by Peruvian archaeologists who laughed his stones out of court – though no one had ever had them scientifically analysed. Now he began to search for the 'depot', and spent whole nights at a

[58]

[59]

time talking with the Indians. He fell under the spell of another world, a world which, according to him, went back at least 100,000 years. He neglected his career as college lecturer in medicine – which brought about all sorts of tensions and difficulties and led finally to his divorce. He became a 'crackpot with crazy ideas', and came up with all sorts of wild and confused theories about a form of genetic engineering that had been practised thousands of years ago and an 'earlier humanity that had contact with extraterrestrials'.

Where are the 'depots'?

At the beginning of the seventies, Cabrera possessed some larger pieces of rock – by larger I mean about 1.5 metres high – on which flying machines were clearly depicted. Not aeroplanes of the kind we are familiar with, but strange flying contraptions in the sky, similar to those found in ancient Indian texts and described by the Indologist Lutz Gentes in his factual yet exciting book.[4] (The same thing is described from the point of view of Vedic religion by the author Armin Risi.[5]) I had the opportunity to admire these rocks with my own eyes, but they were then collected by military lorries and transported to Lima. The Peruvian airforce was planning to set up a museum about the history of flight, and Cabrera's rocks showed strange and ancient flying machines. The Museo Aeronautico is now in the military section of Lima airport, inaccessible to the general public. I haven't been able to find out if Cabrera's rocks adorn the rooms of this museum or not. I assume that they do, though, because they were subjected to analysis before being accepted into the collection.

Apart from the engraved stones, there were of course the clay figures as well, which I want to discuss here. Dr Cabrera is now 77 years old, and has become wary of others, not knowing whom he can really trust. He still receives single tourists or tour groups, shows his collection of stones and interprets them in his own eccentric way. But even someone like myself, who has known Cabrera for a few decades, has difficulty following his stories. And stories is the right word, for they do not fit in with any scientific scheme of things. The old man also uses engravings which he must know are fake to substantiate his beliefs. Why? Has he become so enamoured of his own theories that he thinks imitations will back them up? I had the chance to sit down and talk with Dr Cabrera in a calm and matter-of-fact way. He claimed to now know the location of the secret 'depot', with its thousands upon thousands of figurines.

'Janvier,' I said, 'no one will believe you if you don't say where this "depot" is. Can't you at least show *me*?'

Janvier Cabrera looked me up and down before he answered: 'What good would that do you? To prove anything you would have to show the exact location of the depot. But this is exactly what you mustn't do. That would be an abuse of my trust, and would set the Indians against you. You'd have to get out of Peru quick. And your scientific community? They'll just have a good laugh about it! They'll declare that the whole thing is a huge deception; and no one will want to have anything to do with it. Since they'll think it's all a swindle, no one will care either if the figures are smashed to pieces and destroyed.'

Janvier Cabrera looked at me bitterly. And somehow he was right. From my own experience I know how easy it is to find yourself the subject of mockery if no absolute proof is available. And sometimes even if it is!

I tried to get more out of him, asked him to say more about this 'depot'. I finally learned that the river Ica had, over thousands of years, eroded diverse geological layers, and in the process brought the first engraved stones to light. And the 'depot'? Cabrera thought that the Peruvian archaeologists must know something about such depots, for the first one had been discovered by none other than Julio Caesar Tello, the founder of Peruvian archaeology. In the Serro Corrado, a range of Andes foothills beyond Paracas, Tello had come across several granite caves containing Indian textiles. Access to these caves was gained only through a vertical 6-metre-deep shaft. The caves themselves measured roughly 5 by 7 by 3 metres.

'And in such a cave you found the clay figures?'

Cabrera nodded, and added that there were still 10,000 or so of them there. Not just in one, but in several granite caves. I was dubious. Granite? Here, in this region? The town of Ica was surrounded by a desert of stone and sand that stretched to Nazca and beyond. Of course there were the foothills of the Andes, parts of which were granite, but they were a good distance to the east. I couldn't be sure – I'm not a geologist. Cabrera noticed my hesitation.

'You don't believe that there are gigantic, man-made constructions of granite under the desert sands?'

'I have difficulty imagining it,' I said, rather troubled.

'Then go to Nazca – you know your way round there at least – and climb down into one of the *puquios*!'

'Into one of the *what*?'

'Puquios,' repeated Cabrera. 'The ancient underground water systems around Nazca. No one knows how old they are, but they are still working to this day. They were partly hollowed out of the granite, partly strengthened by mighty granite monoliths. You will see that there are plenty of shafts, vaults and kilometre-long puquios of granite.'

I did what he suggested. But before I relate what I found, I want to return to another subject – the collection of clay figures. Were they ancient and therefore genuine? The relics of an earlier civilization?

Scientific questions

Back in Switzerland I asked Dr Waldemar A Keller of the Geographical Institute at the University of Zurich to analyse the sample I had broken off from a clay figure. A few weeks later I received the devastating result:

Dear Mr Däniken,

You sent us the following sample for radiocarbon dating.
Origin: Ica, Peru.
Code:
Material: unfired clay.

We have registered this sample as UZ-3937/ETH-16012.
It produced a C14 reading of *modern*.

Yours sincerely

Dr W A Keller

The preparation of the sample material necessary for determining its age took place in the radiocarbon laboratory of the Geographical Institute of the University of Zurich. The dating was carried out by means of AMS technology (Accelerator Mass Spectrometry), in the tandem accelerator of the Institute for Particle Physics at the Swiss Institute of Technology (ETH) in Hönggerberg.

So Cabrera's collection was fake. Unfired clay, modern, from our time. These scientists were renowned throughout the world for the care and accuracy of their carbon datings. While I was still pondering why on earth Cabrera was going in for forgery on such a massive scale, my eye fell upon an accompanying letter which Dr Keller had kindly sent me. Suddenly I stopped short. Obviously things weren't completely cut and dried after all. The letter read as follows:

> The preparatory examinations included electronmicroscopic, radio-spectroscopic and other element-specific analyses. The typical composition shows, as was expected, a ceramic-clay combination. In other words, mainly magnesium/aluminium silicates with a relatively high iron content. In addition, besides quartz inclusions, there were also ones with a high calcium and phosphor content (possibly calcium-phosphate particles). The element-analysis showed us that there was enough carbon in the sample to allow radiocarbon dating, so that age could be ascertained through the AMS method. Since this material, as you mentioned in your letter, is unfired clay, *I am still not clear where this carbon derives from, or at what point in time and under what circumstances it was combined with the sample material.* Perhaps your own knowledge and experience will be able to throw more light on the matter.[6]

This made me ponder. On the one hand there was enough carbon material to enable a dating to be completed, on the other hand there was a question about where this same carbon had come from. Now C14 dating is based on the assumption that the radioactive isotope of carbon (C) is always present in the atmosphere in constant amounts with the atomic weight 14. This carbon isotope is taken up by all plants, so that it is contained in constant quantities not only in trees, roots and leaves but also in all other living organisms. All radioactive materials are subject to a particular period of decay – which starts with death in the human being and animal kingdoms, and with harvest or burning in the plant world. The carbon isotope C14 has a half-life of 5,600 years. This means that 5,600 years after the death of an organism only half the original C14 quantity can still be measured, after 11,200 years only a quarter, or after 22,400 years only an eighth. Our present instruments can measure traces up to 30,000 years old.

The measurements carried out by Zurich University gave the result as *modern* carbon – in other words, it contained the full amount of C14 isotopes. But where did this carbon come from? As I was speaking to Dr Keller on the phone I suddenly remembered the cockroaches which had been swarming around Cabrera's figures. Cockroaches! Their excrement contained masses of modern carbon. Had this affected the dating?

But there was another thing. The Ancient Astronaut Society, an international charitable society concerned with the possibility that extraterrestrials visited the earth in prehistoric times, had – independently of me – asked for a second analysis of Cabrera's figures. The geologist Dr Johannes Fiebag had obtained two samples from Dr Cabrera and handed them to his colleague Dr Ernst Freyburg for testing. Dr Freyburg carried out an exhaustive analysis at the University of Weimar. His report reads as follows:

The two samples (internal reference UF6 and UF7) each contained the same amounts of quartz, potassium- and sodium-feldspar, and the clay minerals illite and muscovite. The sample UF6 also contained the clay-minerals kaolinite and montmorillonite. In all, this is a typical clay-mineral composition. The outer crust also contained calcite, alongside the minerals already mentioned. The multiple radiodiagram demonstrates an unsteady base-line of the individual curves as proof of a certain amount of radioamorphic (=glassy) substance.

Differential Thermo Analysis (DTA) determines the loss of mass of a sample at between 20 and 1,000 degrees Celsius. In the present material, at the lower temperature range up to 200 degrees, there is a loss of mass of 1.4 per cent, due both to the residual water content and to a portion of the water hydrate of the clay minerals.

At 424 and at 534 degrees Celsius, two exothermal reactions appear, which demonstrate the presence of combustible organic substance. The combustion temperature of lignite is equivalent to this range.

Above 800 degrees Celsius, the DTA graph points to the presence of glass substance, which is confirmed by the radiological findings. Under the electronmicroscope one can ascertain that the glassy areas consist mainly of SiO_2. However the structures cannot be clearly attributed to silicic acid forming organisms.[7]

The summary of the analysis also states that the lighter crust consists of limestone sand, in which the figures had lain after drying out. And the age?

No clear result could be obtained. The existence of a residual water content (though in very small quantities) does however indicate a relatively young age. The presence of carbon would allow a C14 dating to be carried out, but this would only ascertain the age of the carbon.

So where were we now? As Goethe said:

So here I am, poor fool, once more,
And know as much as I did before![8]

The University of Zurich says the sample is 'modern', but this might be the result of cockroach droppings. The University of Weimar reserves judgement, but ascertains that there are 'very small quantities' of residual water content. This does not, however, have to be 'residual water', but could be the result of damp conditions in Cabrera's 'depot'.

Young and fake or old and genuine?

I personally find it hard to believe that Cabrera's figurines are extremely old. Yet the dating results are more confusing than they at first appear. Have I judged wrongly? One of the most widespread illnesses is diagnosis. What are the arguments in favour of Cabrera's whole collection being fake?

• Cabrera's eccentricity, coupled with a certain obstinacy that has increased with age.

• His antagonism towards archaeology, the Peruvian variety in particular.

- His sense of national identity: he would like 'his' country to have been something exceptional from Noah's day onwards.

- His conviction that a much older civilization existed before ours.

- The figures themselves: why should an earlier civilization store their knowledge in granite caves in the form of unfired clay figures?

- The clearly identifiable forgeries of today – both of clay figures and engraved stones. I'm referring to the motifs which could not possibly be 30,000 or more years old – such as copies of the scrape drawings on the Nazca plain, or a 'Moses-like' figure with two 'stone tablets' in his hands.

And is there anything to set against these rock-solid arguments, any glimmer of possibility that the figures might, after all, be genuine? Yes! Though some of the above points seem intractable, others might have an explanation. For example, the question about how a 'Moses-like' figure could have arrived in Cabrera's collection might be illumined from the following angle:

The 'Bible' of the Mormons, a religious community based mainly in the USA, is called the *Book of Mormon*. To it belong the 24 sheets of the Book of Esther, which deal with the history of the Jared people. The Jaredites are supposed to have left Mesopotamia at the time the tower of Babel was built – whenever that was. In two strange ships, illuminated day and night by 16 'shining stones', they reached South America. They achieved this by following the directions of the 'highest Lord, who came from the clouds', and who not only taught them the art of shipbuilding, but also gave them the compass.

The Jaredites were the ancestors of the Mormons. Their trek from the coast of present-day Chile to Central and finally North America, took many thousands of years. These immigrants could quite possibly have known the story of Moses, as well as other things from a far-distant past. They might well have made Moses-figures and other statuettes, and concealed them somewhere. What I can't imagine, though, is that this should have happened tens of thousands of years ago.

There are various arguments in support of the figures' authenticity:

- The number of them. Cabrera's collection alone consists of more than 2,500 pieces.

● The repetition of identical or very similar depictions. On one rack I found 12 'tennis rackets' together. Another rack contained about 30 more of these 'saucepan lids with handles'. If Cabrera had ordered the forgeries, why should he want 30 of the same at one go? What good would it do him?

● The fact that Cabrera never sells his figures but guards them jealously.

● The pictures of surgery. I photographed a whole series of these and they do not accord with modern medical knowledge. Cabrera, who is after all an emeritus professor of surgery, must know all the processes involved in an operation. Why should the hypothetical forgers show something quite different?

● The scenes of homosexual sex. These appear in both the engraved stones and clay figures. Cabrera himself hates homosexuality and would never ask for such scenes to be portrayed, let alone pay for them![60]

● Cabrera's divorce from his wife. She demanded half the stone engravings and figures. Cabrera went to the highest court in the land

71

to avoid handing over any of his collection to his ex-wife. Would he have bothered if they were fake? And why should his wife want half of a fake and worthless collection?

● The related motifs in other similar collections, thousands of miles away from Ica, including:

a) The Acambaro collection in Mexico. Hundreds of clay figures with motifs similar to the ones in Cabrera's collection, including dinosaurs.

b) The collection of the late priest Crespi in Cuenca, Ecuador. Whole rooms full of figurines made of wood and clay.[61, 62] Also engraved metal sheets. Similar motifs are depicted, including dinosaurs;

c) The figures in 'Burrows' Cave': in 1982 Russel Burrows found a cave system 'somewhere in Illinois', whose exact location is known only to a very few people.[9] There are two books which reproduce the figurines found there.[10,11] Many of them are similar to the objects in Cabrera's collection.

d) The thousands of 'anthropomorphic' stone and clay figures found throughout Japan, often depicting human-animal creatures. They can be seen in many different Japanese museums. A book of photographs of them is available.[12] Many of them are very similar to Cabrera's figures.

e) Clay figures, like the ones in the Cabrera collection, which have been found in several towns in Ecuador (Valdivia, Agua Blanca, Chirije, San Isodoro, La Tolita). They also include human-animal creatures.[13]

f) Dinosaur and human footprints in *the same* layer of stone, found in the Paluxy River near Glen Rose in Texas.[14]

And these are by no means all. I personally know of a whole number of private collections in South and Central America which show similar motifs. These private collections can't really be counted, because each owner is convinced his figures are genuine and, like Cabrera, doesn't want the authorities to start meddling. Somewhere in the world there must be a whole horde of fakers at work, continually creating similar

[61]

[62]

figures! This mafia of forgers must also have made secret arrangements with the Indians in Ecuador, Peru, Mexico and the USA, and with the many private collectors, to ensure the motifs on their forgeries are all more or less in line with each other – including the human-animal figures and the dinosaurs.

To argue about the age of the various collections won't at present get us very far. What astonishes me, though, is that in the last four years various discoveries have come to light which call into doubt current theories about the continuous evolution of the human race.

Arguments for 'tens of thousands of years'

1 White Bear, an old Hopi Indian, tells the history of his clan, which is supposed to reach back *hundreds of thousands* of years.[15] The Sioux chief White Wolf says the same thing. Presently in his nineties, he even says that the history of the indigenous North American population stretches back four million years.[16]

2 Dr Richard Thompson and Dr Michael Cremo created a furore in the USA with their two weighty volumes of exposé. In *Forbidden Archaeology*, volumes 1 and 2, they offer proof that the cultural legacy of humanity reaches back more than 100,000 years.[17]

3 In 1994, in the Rhone valley, the 'Chauvet caves' were discovered. They contained a stone-age art gallery depicting surreal 'monsters' as well as animal motifs. There were also 'heads which remind one of dinosaurs', as well as 'birdmen'.[18] These works of art have been dated at 32,000 years old. The French archaeologist Michel Lorblanchet said that 'Chauvet is just the tip of the iceberg. There must have been other stages, preparatory to the one which found expression here, of which we are still ignorant.'

4 The Romanian cave-diver Christian Lascu discovered the remains of a cult site that is said to be 70,000–85,000 years old, in a limestone cave in the Bihor mountains.[19] He found bones there which were arranged in the form of a cross pointing to the four directions.

5 Sixty kilometres east of Carson City, Nevada, USA, the oldest mummy of North America was found. It has been dated at 100,000 years old. Where there is a mummy, there must also have been a culture that it belonged to.[20]

6 In the Caverna de Pedra Pintada near Santarem (north Brazil), cave paintings from 12,000 BC were found. Among them was a human figure with the head of an insect. Cabrera's collection boasts a similar design.

7 In September 1996, Dr Lesley Head of the University of Wollongong in Australia (150 kilometres south of Sydney) announced that 176,000-year-old signs and pictures etched in stone, as well as tools, had been found. The place where they were found lies at the edge of the Kimberley plateau in northwest Australia, east of Kununurra. The *Sydney Morning Herald* even reported that giant stone sculptures, reminiscent of Stonehenge in England, had been discovered.[21] There were also several thousand inscriptions, estimated to be up to 75,000 years old. In the Kimberley mountains there are no end of prehistoric rock paintings, among them 'mythological creatures' and figures with 'halos' round their heads.

8 In the Museo Padre le Paige in San-Pedro-de-Atacama in Chile, one can see clay figures that could have come straight from Cabrera's collection. Their age is uncertain – and in some cases hotly debated. The priest Le Paige, who has since died, dedicated his life to Chilean archaeology. Half a year before he died he said in an interview that he had found underground vaults containing skeletons and figures which were over 100,000 years old. His words were:

> I believe that extraterrestrial beings were also buried there. Some of the mummies I found had facial forms almost unknown on earth. People would not believe me if I related what else I found in the graves![22]

These are only some of the reports which I have added to my archives in the past few years. Not only are the datings astounding, reaching back much further than has ever been imagined, but also the motifs. Why, 10,000 kilometres apart from each other, does one find similar depictions of 'birdmen', human-animal creatures, and even dinosaurs – although no human being can ever have seen a dinosaur? What on earth was going on in the heads of our stone-age forefathers? I'm no longer surprised by the naive solutions of archaeologists: they carry on snoozing in their blissful dream-world, in their psychological, shaman-jungle of misconceptions. This may satisfy them – but not me. The French archaeologist Michel Lorblanchet, for example, who studied the paintings at Chauvet, believed that these stone-age artists can only have 'dreamt up such fantastic visions in a state of trance'.[23] According to him these visions stem 'directly from the subconscious'.

Cabrera's clay figures could be fake, or a mixture of fake and very ancient, genuine motifs. I don't wish to pass final judgement on the matter, yet questions still remain. Why do so many different figure collections reveal such closely related designs? And where do the forgers get their ideas from? The Peruvian Indians cannot, after all, get inspiration from millennia-old rock paintings in France. And the French stone-age artists can hardly have gone to Australia to get ideas.

I can imagine that Cabrera's figures could have been produced by a school. Children might have made in clay what they had been taught about in history. This would account for the numerous repetitions, with small variations. It is quite possible that in prehistoric Peru there were also other art forms, quite different from the clay figures: textiles, for example, or a kind of 'paper' like that used by the Mayas in Central America. The textiles which have survived the millennia actually do show motifs similar to the figures, but the hypothetical 'paper' of course did not survive. What remains are a few caves full of clay figures, made by a group of children and youths – a school of some sort, in other words.

The pictures towards the end of this book are intended to further stimulate debate about Cabrera's collection. They may provoke comparison with other collections of which I am unaware.

And what about the puquios, the underground water channels around Nazca? Do they exist? Are they, at least, ancient beyond any doubt? And if so, who were the engineers who built them?

The first person in Nazca I asked about the puquios was Eduardo Herran, the chief pilot of Aero Condor. I've known him for more than 30 years, and he knows the whole area like the back of his hand.

'You want to see puquios? Follow me!'

We flew over the Nazca valley with its thin thread of a stream that flows down from the Andes. Eduardo pointed out to me a series of round holes in the ground, which came to meet each other from two directions. They reminded me of great eyes, growing in spiral fashion out of the ground.[63]

'Here are your puquios,' laughed Eduardo. 'There are 29 of them in the Nazca valley, two in the Taruga valley and four in the valley of Las Trancas. It's astonishing that they still work, providing fresh water – no one has altered them for centuries.'

'Are they water holes, a kind of deep well?'

'More than that,' explained Eduardo. 'The holes you can see from up here are only the access places to fresh water. Below them are stone pipes through which the water flows. No one knows for how many kilometres these underground pipes extend.'

[63]

'And when were they made?' I asked.

Eduardo told me I should ask the experts. As far as he knew, he said, there was controversy about when they had been built – every researcher had his own opinion. The Indians themselves had different views again. The local population believed that beneath the Cerro Blanco – a 2,500-metre-high mountain not far from Nazca, and known for the enormous sand dune which covers its upper portion – was a great lake, from which the water in the puquios flowed. One legend says that the creator god Viracocha made the puquios. Long long ago, when the region had dried out and the inhabitants were going hungry, the Indians prayed fervently to Viracocha. They cried and shouted the word 'nana', which is equivalent to 'pain and woe' in the Kechua language. This word 'nana' later became the name 'Nazca'. The whole population had made a pilgrimage to the foot of Cerro Blanco – for this was their holy mountain, where they had always prayed to the gods. Then Viracocha had come down to them in fire and smoke, and seeing the torment of his people had himself begun to cry. His tears formed a great lake beneath Cerro Blanco, and he conducted its waters by means of underground channels and puquios.

Nothing but a legend. Yet it is somehow reminiscent of the Israelites and the god who descended to them on Mount Sinai. In addition, no one I have asked understands why the largest sand dune in the world sits on top of Cerro Blanco. Sand piles of this enormous size are not usually found on top of high mountains. If there is sand it is usually blown away, or overlaid by snow or water. The sand then turns into sandstone or green undergrowth starts to sprout from it. But not on Cerro Blanco. Is it not possible then, that there really were gullies which conducted the water from Cerro Blanco down into an underground cavern?

Who were these engineers?

We rented a jeep – myself and my friends Uli Dopatka and Valentin Nussbaumer – and set off to find the puquios. As usual the sun was blazing down mercilessly on the dried-up landscape and there were no

roads to speak of. At last, worn out after several wrong turnings and long hikes on foot, we stood before the first puquio. A perfectly graded spiral led downwards. At its widest point it was 12.70 metres in diameter. Lumps of stone of various sizes formed a cleanly built wall, which made a footpath to the next level down. At its deepest point, 5.30 metres below the surface, a stream burbled through a man-made water channel that was roofed with a granite monolith.[64–66]

One after another we plunged our hands into the stream. The water was fresh and clean – in contrast to the local Nazca river which stank to high heaven and was full of all kinds of rubbish. The next spiral lay another 70 metres further on, after which there were five more at intervals of a few hundred metres. All were wells of fresh water, from an unknown source, laid down by a people for whom it must have been of enormous importance to have fresh water at that particular spot. This may sound obvious, but it isn't if you know the region. Nazca's neighbouring valleys are the Ingenio and Palpa, through both of which flows more water than there is in the so-called Nazca 'river'.

[65]

[66]

What was there to stop a small tribe of Indians who wanted to go in for some modest cultivation from settling in the neighbouring valleys? Or from finding an Andes valley 50 kilometres to the east, where there was fresh water in abundance? Why was it so important to settle in this unpromising wilderness of Nazca? Nomadic peoples never think in an impractical way. Water is the prerequisite for any settlement. But here there was either none or very little – either way there was too little. This is proven by the need for an underground water system around Nazca. So this particular point in the desert must have had some other attraction. It must have been unique in some way – so much so that the settlement *had* to be here, even though it meant building the puquios to supply water. This reminds me of the oldest Maya town in Central America, Tikal. There also there was a shortage of water, yet this didn't prevent the building of a great metropolis with thousands of buildings and more than 70 pyramids. Why didn't the Mayas settle 40 kilometres away, on the Peten-Itza lake? Because the site of Tikal was holy: the 'family of heaven' was supposed to have settled here originally.[24] This site therefore became a place of pilgrimage. So the town had to be here and nowhere else! And because there was no water to speak of, kilometre-long water channels and giant underground reservoirs were built.

I suspect that it was the same in Nazca. There is no good reason why an Indian tribe should settle in a barren part of the country – unless it was for a religious reason. Which religion? Did the trail-like lines of Nazca have something to do with it? Such an underground water system exists only in the region of Nazca – and the 'experts' also state this.[25]

And how were the underground channels built?

Uli, Valentin and I helped each other crawl as far as we could into individual channels. The 'pipes' as well as the access holes were of varying kinds of construction. Sometimes stone spirals led down into the depths, and the pipes lay in an artificial bed of cleanly carved stone, covered with granite slabs. At other places the access hole was a shaft dug straight down into the ground without supporting stone slabs.[67, 68] The pipe was always at a depth of about 6 metres below ground. And in every case the actual water channels were artificially

[67]

[68]

made pipes, rather than natural water courses. The specialist literature gives varying dimensions for these channels: 50 centimetres broad and 70 high, or 70 by 70 centimetres.[26] Just large enough for a man bending down. Two of these pipes run without doubt under the bed of the Rio de Nazca.[27] No one knows their course after that. But one is forced to ask how and why they did this. Why did the builders of this system lay down a water channel under the bed of a river? There were several puquios on both sides of the river. And how did prehistoric Indians with their simple tools and sealing methods manage to construct this wonder of engineering? Did they drain the river bed? Hardly. So they must have dug a tunnel, as in mining. But the water seeping through from the river above ought to have made tunnelling well-nigh impossible.

There's another curious thing: the Spanish conquerors knew nothing about the origin of either the figures and lines on the Nazca plain, or the underground water system. So the underground network must have been there before they arrived. Various experts have attempted to date it – with varying results: anything from AD 1,400 back to

[69]

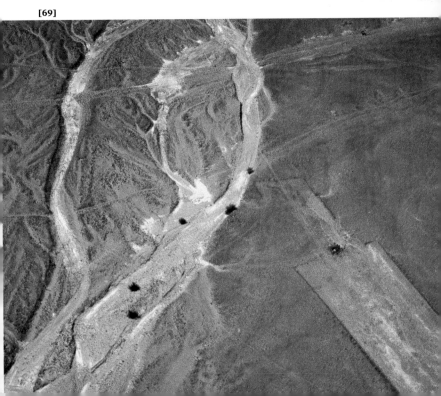

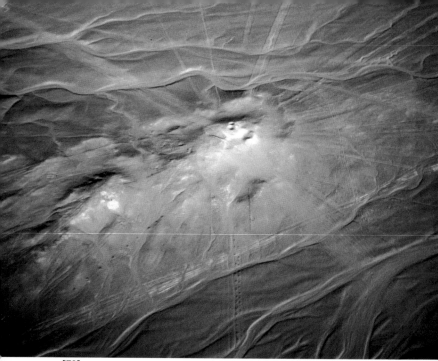

[70]

the grey dawn of time. It is even possible that the network of water channels under the ground is far older than the access holes above.[28, 29] Only one thing is certain: in the Nazca region there exists a huge underground network of canals ('una verdadera red subterránea'[30]). The technology that made it is unknown, yet is 'unique in Peru and probably all America'.[31] Is it possible that this network had something to do not only with the supply of fresh water, but also the runways and lines? It cannot be discounted. By the beginning of the forties, Alberto Rossel Castro had discovered three puquios together between the Rio Grande and the Pan-Americana Highway, the main road running from north to south. They bear the names Achako, Anklia and San Marcelo. The puquio San Marcelo lies 10 metres below the surface between the Aja and Tierra Blanca streams, which have water only at certain times of the year. But it is at this very spot that the first Nazca lines begin. The short, sporadic flooding of the streams touches only the very edge of the runways at most. Does this floodwater seep down into an underground collection system? Kurpe, another water pipe on the east

[71]

[72]

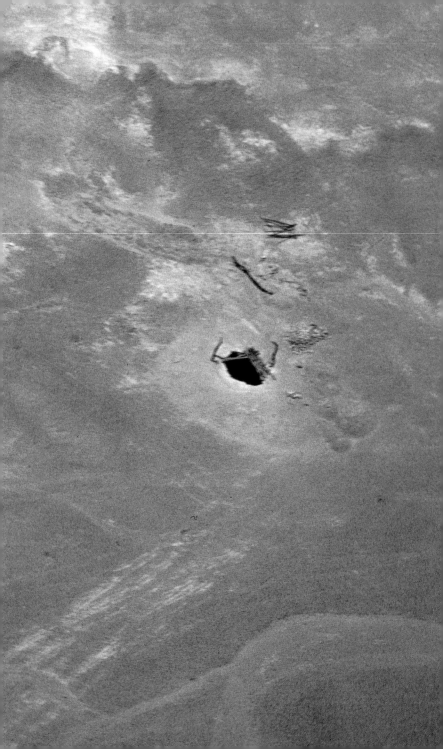

side of the road, lies near foothills yet is still within the area of the Nazca lines. Its access hole measures a full 20 metres across.

On the desert surface of Nazca there are two places (perhaps more – I only know these two) where many different lines from all points of the compass meet. And in the middle, where they join, there is a yawning hole in the ground.[71-73] The entrance to a puquio? I would love to have had myself lowered from a helicopter to take a closer look at one of them. Unfortunately there's no chance of this happening – you can't get permission for such things.

So what are we to make of the riddle of Nazca? Is any single one of the many Nazca theories the right one? Or have we all missed something important?

Notes

1 Erich von Däniken, proofs, London, New York, 1977.

2 Janvier Cabrera-Darquien, *El Mensaje de la Piedras Grabadas de Ica*, Lima, 1976.

3 Erich von Däniken, op. cit.

4 Lutz Gentes, *Die Wirklichkeit der Götter. Raumfahrt im frühen Indien*, Munich/Essen, 1996.

5 Armin Risi, *Gott und die Götter. Das vedische Weltbild revolutioniert die moderne Wissenschaft*, Esoterik und Theologie, Zurich/Berlin, 1995.

6 Dating completed by the Geographical Institute of the Zurich-Irchel University on 16 July 1996. Letter from Dr Waldemar A Keller of the same date.

7 Ernst Freyburg, 'Mineralogische Untersuchung an Feststein- und Tonfigurproben aus Peru', *Scientific Ancient Skies*, vol. 2, 1995.

8 Translation by M Barton.

9 Luc Bürgin, 'Burrow's Cave – eine sensationelle Entdeckung in America?', *Fremde aus dem All*, Munich, 1995.

10 R Burrows and F Rydholm, *The Mystery Cave of Many Faces*, Marquette, 1992.

11 J Scherz and R Burrows, *Rock Art Pieces from Burrows' Cave*, Marquette, 1992.

12 Illegible Japanese title, copyright Kodansha, Japan, NDC 210.

13 'Entre tiestos y restauradores', *El Comercio*, 23 May 1996.

14 Cecil N Dougherty, *Valley of the Giants*, Clebirne, Texas, 1971.

15 Joseph F Blumrich, *Kasskara und die sieben Welten – Weisser Bär erzählt den Erdmythos der Hopi-Indianern*, Dusseldorf, 1979.

16 Sioux chief White Wolf, *Ancient Skies*, vol. 23, no. 1, Highland Park, Illinois, 1996.

17 Richard Thompson and Michael A Cremo, *Forbidden Archaeology*, Essen, 1994.

18 'Geisterzeichen in der Tiefe', *Der Spiegel*, no. 50, 1996.

19 Ibid.

20 'Tasche mit Asche', *Der Spiegel*, no. 19, 1996.

21 'Spektakulärer Fund von Skulpturen in Westaustralien', *Neue Zürcher Zeitung*, 23 September 1996.

22 Erich von Däniken, *Reise nach Kiribati*, Dusseldorf, 1982, p.170.

23 'Geisterzeichen in der Tiefe', Der Spiegel, no. 50, 1996.

24 Erich von Däniken, *Der Tag, an dem die Götter kamen*, Munich, 1984, chapter 1.

25 Katherine Schreiber and Josué Lancho Rojas, 'Los puquios de Nazca: un sistema de galerias filtrantes', *Boletin de Lima*, no. 59, September 1988.

26 Alberto P Rossel Castro, 'Sistema de irrigacion antigua de Rio Grande de Nazca', *Revista del Museo Nacional*, Lima, vol. 11, no. 2, 1942.

27 Anthony Aveni, 'The Lines of Nazca', *Memoirs of the American Philosophical Society*, vol. 193, 1990.

28 Persis B Clarkson and I Roland Dorn, 'New Chronometric Dates for the Puquios of Nazca', *Latin American Antiquity*, vol. 6, no. 1, 1995.

29 *Acueductos y caminos antiguos de la hoya del Rio Grande de Nazca*, Actas y Trabajos Cientificos del XXVII Congreso 1939, vol. 1, Congreso International de Americanistas, Lima, pp. 559–69.

30 Rossel Castro, op. cit.

31 Schreiber and Lancho Rojas, op. cit.

3

WHAT HAPPENED IN NAZCA?

*The difference between God and the
historians consists above all in the fact
that God cannot alter the past.*
SAMUEL BUTLER, 1835–1902

O n the red rack in my office, directly in my line of vision, are
piled 102 books, magazines and brochures about Nazca. I
have ploughed my way through all of them, covered them
with coloured marks, and scribbled notes in their margins. Nazca
without end! Theory after theory. And many an author just adopts
the opinion of another, so that it becomes obvious to anyone who
knows anything about the subject that the writer in question can never
have set foot in Nazca – unless of course he sacrificed his precious
time to make a brief tourist visit. Nor does science come up with
anything we can be sure about, even though the tone of the relevant
scientific publications makes it sound as though everything had been
cleared up long ago.

At last – so I read in the scientific magazine *Nature* – dating has
been successfully established.[1] How? In the heat, a fine film containing
manganese oxide, traces of iron and clay minerals, forms around the
small stones. Below the stone, however, lichen, moulds and cyano
bacteria develop – organic material, in other words. So all one needs
to do is find stones which were removed from their original position by
the makers of the Nazca lines, and then date the organic traces
beneath them with C14 methods. The lichen and moulds do not form
in conditions of burning heat, but rather on the shadow side of the
stone. Now there is no shortage of stones at the edge of runways in
Nazca, stones which, according to the scientists, must have been

removed by the line makers. Since then they have apparently stayed where they were put, enabling lichen and mould to grow beneath them. So a test was carried out on *nine* stones collected from the edge of a Nazca line or runway. The dating showed an age between 190 BC and AD 600. The newspaper *Neue Zürcher Zeitung* reported: 'In this way results were obtained which accorded fairly precisely with the purely stylistic dating of Nazca pottery remains.'[2]

This method may be a good idea. But how can one be sure that the nine stones tested were really removed by the original line makers and have never been touched since? Perhaps, 1,800 years ago, pre-Inca tourists strolled over the pampa and shifted stones with their sandals from the edge of the lines to somewhere else. Of course this doesn't necessarily make the results null and void – but does this dating hold good for the first and oldest of all the runways?

Professor Anthony Aveni, anthropologist and astronomer at the Colgate University in America, apparently knows exactly what happened at Nazca: 'We now know the identity of the line markers,' he writes, then proceeds to cast doubt upon Maria Reiche's ideas.[3] Reiche, he says, identified many of the animal figures as star-charts, correlating, for example, the monkey with the Lion and Plough constellations, and the spider with Orion. Yet he believes her ideas had too little to say about the actual people who created these figures. He says that such a people still exists, and points to present-day Cuzco. There, high in the Andes, a pre-Inca system of lines can actually be found. The local Indians there call it *ceques* – a network of visible and invisible lines that converge on Cuzco from all directions. The 'ceque-system' around Cuzco is connected with the calendar, water supply and mountain gods, and yearly ceremonies still take place today upon particular lines. Aveni superimposes these facts on Nazca, believing that there are geometrical connections between the lines and underground water courses. According to him, then, the Nazca Indians had rituals and line markings connected with their water supply, in the same way that the Cuzco Indians still have today. Then he asks whether the Nazca lines might, in addition to their ritual purpose, have served as roads of some kind – meaning paths and sites for ceremonies, and ritual dances. Aveni even suggests that the lines and geometrical markings in Nazca might perhaps have served to mark out an area of work done in honour of the gods. One thing he says we can at last be sure of is that the people of Nazca made the Nazca lines. Really? Well, who else would have made them?

To sum up his point of view, then, the Indians sought out certain areas to carry out their ceremonies. The straight, narrow lines indicated the course of water – seen as holy – both above and below ground; and the geometrical figures arose as places of worship to some gods or other. Professor Helaine Silverman, co-author of the Aveni article, had previously written a scientific treatise of her own, in which she propounded that the scrape drawings around Nazca were the tribal symbols of various Indian clans.[4] In principle I have nothing against this sort of view, but how, one must ask, can the various Indian communities have recognized their own and other symbols? They can, after all, only be recognized from the air – and not, as is continually suggested, from some mountain or other. I am talking about the figures on the pampa now, not the runways and long lines.

The American professor Dr Aldon Mason, an archaeologist who specializes in South America, has written pages and pages about the ceramics and textiles to be found between Paracas and Nazca. One stripe or two more, a different colour – and you're talking, apparently, about a quite different style and community. 'The absence of blue and green is worthy of note. The motifs fall into two main categories: naturalistic-zoomorphous, and mythological depictions.'[5] One learns that the Nazca graves were bottle-like in shape, with an upper shaft and a depth of up to 5 metres. (This reminds me immediately of Cabrera's 'depot'.) 'Many of the Nazca skulls show a deformity of length,' notes Professor Mason.

This observation deserves our attention. (In the Ica museum there are two such skulls.) I have been asking myself for years why people would want to torture their infants by lengthening and thus deforming their still-soft skull bones. If this custom was confined to Peru one might dismiss it as a local aberration. But no – deformed skulls have been found as far afield as North America, Mexico, Ecuador, Bolivia, Chile, Patagonia, Oceania, the European steppes, central and western

Africa, Brittany, and of course Egypt. And now, as Professor Mason tells us, they have been found in Nazca graves.

What kind of perversion was it that made our forefathers want to squash their children's heads and lengthen them? Archaeologists speak of a kind of 'utilitarian thinking' which saw such deformity as useful in some way, perhaps for wearing head gear which enabled them to carry loads more easily. I don't believe a word of it. A normal head is better equipped for carrying loads than one which has been pulled longways out of shape. Another idea is that such deformity might have represented some ideal of beauty, or that it served to distinguish one social class from another.

I have another point of view. Human beings have always been great imitators, orientating themselves in accordance with some ideal or model. These skull deformations are nothing other than an unnatural 'beautifying', a horrific example of human vanity so widespread in prehistoric times that it became truly international.

But *who* was being imitated? All around the globe, people had encountered the imposing gods. And everywhere, imitators who wanted to look big modelled themselves – at least outwardly – on these beings. The priests quickly got hold of the idea of seeming godlike by having long skulls. That was an easy way to gain influence over others!

So I am not in the least astonished by deformed skulls in the graves of Nazca. I would have been surprised if none had been found. They fit in with the whole picture of the region, like the zoomorphous figurines or the textiles with mystical designs.

And two neurologists – brain and nerve specialists, in other words – have given me something else to think about: it is quite feasible to press the soft bones of an infant's skull, day after day, between two boards, until the head is two or three times longer than a normal head. But *brain capacity* is not altered one iota. The size of the brain is not affected by the deformation. The rest of the lengthened skull simply fills with fluid. The child will either not live long or suffer from hydrocephalus.

All deformed skulls so far discovered throughout the world have simply been catalogued. No exact research – from a new angle – has ever been carried out. Everything has always seemed so clear and self-explanatory. But what if at least some of these skulls are not of earthly origin?

Professor Aldon Mason says of the scrape drawings around Nazca: 'They were without doubt created for the eyes of heavenly deities.' At last, a sensible idea!

The litany of cults

Only large publishing houses can regularly afford to produce opulent coffee-table books. The target audience for such publications is mainly a younger readership. In one of these illustrated volumes about the lines of Nazca, you can read that some authors – meaning me! – think the lines were made by extraterrestrials. Yet to support such a hypothesis, says this book, 'one would have to overlook certain established facts' and assume that beings of higher intelligence had 'flown with the speed of light and used the Nazca desert as a space airport'.[6]

This is just the old regurgitated nonsense that infects more than half of the specialist literature. One author adopts it from another and, hey presto, it's supposed to be true. Let me make two points. Firstly, the speed of light is *not* necessary for interstellar space travel – nor even half or a tenth of it. One or two per cent of the speed of light is enough. And experts think this will be quite possible in the near future.[7,8] And secondly, I have never, anywhere, stated that the Nazca desert was a 'space airport'.

The same author, the archaeologist Simone Waisbard, goes on to say that most Peruvian experts agree that 'the drawings of Nazca are an astronomical calendar'.[9] Hmm! She says that the Nazca people had a hard struggle for survival, which necessitated the construction of great irrigation systems. General opinion, she says, inclines to the idea that 'the giant picture book of Nazca was meant to help determine the amounts of rainfall that were to be expected'. Still today, she goes on, many farmers 'read the stars for indications of rainfall'. And finally, the Nazca Indians probably forecast the weather from the 'flight of seabirds' which resemble the Nazca drawings.

Like many things which are cooked in the scientific pot, such ideas sound very reasonable at first glance. But they are not. Since when have the stars shown anyone how much rain is going to fall? And what about the fact that it never rains in Nazca, and has not done so for millennia? If it had rained, the earth markings would no longer be there. In their struggle to survive, did the Nazca people construct underground water systems? Yes, it's true; the Indians needed water to survive, but why did they settle in a dried-up region when there was more water not far away? And, finally, 'seabirds' have no resemblance whatsoever to the Nazca drawings. So I am left wondering why our young people have to be infected with such nonsense.

The calendar theories too, endlessly regurgitated in archaeological literature, make our ancient forefathers out to have been pretty dumb. This applies equally to our ancestors at Stonehenge, Nazca or anywhere else. The seasons were the most mundane and self-evident thing in the life of stone-age people. Every year there was spring, summer, autumn and winter – and had been since time began. Prehistoric people such as hunters and gatherers knew all the signs of the seasons without the aid of occult mysteries. They could tell when the ground was getting soft, when particular insects started crawling, when the first grasses and plants started to sprout. Stone-age people didn't need any starry hocus pocus to tell them when the berries or other fruits were getting ripe. Of course it *is* possible to see from the constellations, which appear at the same time each year in the firmament, when spring has arrived. But this has nothing to do with important matters like survival.

And of what use could the runways and trapezoid surfaces have been? 'Were they perhaps pens for the holy animals sacrificed to the gods? Plots of land connected to the irrigation tunnels? Observatories? Or sites where the tribes gathered at ritual festivals?'[10]

There is no end to such fantasies – and somehow they're made to sound reasonable suppositions. If the trapezoid surfaces had been 'animal pens', there would have been fences – of which there is no trace.

Nor could they have been 'plots' of agricultural land. It is precisely *because* nothing grew that the trapezoid and runway surfaces are visible. And if they had been sites for ritual festivals would we not still see signs of the dancers' sandal-prints today? There is one thought I try to hold fast to, through all the vagaries of Nazca theory: if this was a site for ritual festivals and dance, why was it just here? Why, for heaven's sake, in this dried-up wilderness? And at the end of the day all these 'sensible solutions' cannot explain why there are zigzag lines *under* certain runways. They do not explain the figures etched on cliff faces, nor why whole mountain summits had to be levelled to make room for a runway as wide as a four-lane highway. These scientific explanations are just unsubstantiated, piecemeal hunches.

In the scientific tome *Weltatlas der alten Kulturen* (World Atlas of Ancient Cultures), the baffled reader can learn that some of the Nazca lines could have been paths 'which had sacred significance, and which were trodden during particular rites and ceremonies'. But their chief purpose was most likely 'as a sacrifice to the ancestors or to gods of the sky and the mountains, who provided the water so essential for cultivation'.[11]

In locally published scientific literature on the subject, everything can be claimed apart from what's staring you in the face. Almost grotesque acrobatics of the mind are carried out to ensure that the boat of received opinion is not rocked. The Nazca Indians must have been absolute buffoons if these theories are to be believed. Let me say it for the hundredth time: *there was no agriculture in the desert and mountain region of Nazca.* The only cultivation was – and still is – carried out in those valleys which are watered by streams from the Andes. We do not know to what extent additional pieces of land were irrigated by the underground water system. But these additional fields would not have had any connection with the runways, lines and figures of Nazca, which have survived the millennia only because nothing sprouted or flowered there.

Albrecht Kottmann has taken a quite different approach to the riddle. He has divided the figures into different units of measurement. For example:

> The picture [of the bird] is 286 metres long. If one divides its length into 22 parts, the body takes up 3, the jagged neck takes 5, the rest of the neck and the head take 2, and the long beak occupies 12 parts. The ratio between the length from tail feathers to the beginning of the beak, and the length of the beak itself, is 5:6. [He suspects that underlying the geometrical drawings there is] a sign language, in which the same words are written, first in gigantic letters, then in minuscule ones.[12]

Perhaps mathematics can help to explain some of the Nazca questions. I'm not in a position to judge. But the division of the figures into subsections still doesn't tell me anything about the runways and zigzag lines.

Nazca theories of a more down-to-earth kind are put forward by the British author Evan Hadingham. Nevertheless he suggests that 'powerful plant hallucinogens' could have been the cause of the Nazca Indians' activity.[13] Not in a month of Sundays. You can't solve geometrical problems with a drug-befuddled brain. Hadingham thinks that the sole key to the riddle is that the lines were a form of worship to the mountain gods. As I will show, the mountain gods are wholly blameless of the Nazca phenomenon.

Academic minds

By now you may well be hoping that we've dealt with all the main theories about Nazca. I'm afraid not – there's still more fun to come! The anthropologist William H Isbell of the New York State University solved all Nazca problems with two words: occupational therapy. He suggested that the Nazca people possessed no facilities for storing agricultural produce. Therefore in times of good harvest the population might have grown too numerous, and would then come close to starvation if a bad harvest came along. What was to be done? 'The solution to the problem lay in maintaining the population's common interest in ceremonial works, which required enough energy to regularly absorb economic excess.' He suggested that it was quite irrelevant whether the Indians could see the results of their occupational therapy or not. It was just 'a way of regulating the population numbers' through work-creation.[14]

I can just imagine it: 'Calorie Priests' – the ones with large skulls of course – running around to check on the amount of energy expended!

The different opinions of the 'experts' all compete with one another: one moment the Indians have laid down underground water systems to irrigate more fields, then suddenly they're hopping around on the ritual sites of the trapezoid surfaces; next moment they're sacrificing to the gods, then taking drugs – even practising birth control through occupational therapy. Nothing seems too wayward or far-fetched to be included in the list of serious possibilities. So let's take the whole thing just one crazy step further: Helmut Tributsch, Professor of Physical Chemistry at the University of Berlin, has solved the Nazca riddle at one blow. He believes that the great prehistoric cult sites were 'always erected at places where mirages appear with particular frequency'.[15] The Professor cites as examples the menhir sites in Brittany, Stonehenge, sacred sites in the Gulf of Mexico, the pyramids of Egypt, and – wait for it – Nazca. Now at last we know what inspired these people to their mysterious works – fata morganas!

Professor Tributsch's view is that above such places there are wonderful 'displays of light and colour' in the sky – mirages of far-distant islands, woods, buildings and lakes reflected in the firmament. The Nazca Indians admired these airy reflections, and because they saw them in the sky, they became 'the other world' for them. Their lines and figures were built in response to this phenomenon. After passing on these words of wisdom, the Berlin scholar proceeds to give me a dressing down: 'Däniken asserts without more ado that the giant runways in the Nazca desert were laid down as landing strips by astronauts of other planets.' He finishes me off – though it leaves me unperturbed – by saying: 'the astronauts, who must have flown through the wide reaches of space, could hardly have relied upon winged aeroplanes for their landing.'[16]

What should I reply? Here is yet another supposed scientist who hasn't bothered to read Däniken. For if he had, he wouldn't disseminate such garbage. I have never written that extraterrestrials 'laid down landing strips', nor have I suggested that the poor ETs had to rely on 'winged aeroplanes for their landing'. Just to refresh everyone's memory: in the ancient holy texts of India there are numerous mentions of aircraft of all sorts. They were called *vimanas*, and were described not just in a general way, but in precise detail.[17, 18] No single one of these flying contraptions covered interstellar distances with the aid of wings. For their earth-exploration sorties, they all exited without exception from the hangar of a mother ship. But this misinterpretation aside, I still can't get to grips with the idea of fata morganas in Nazca. What kind of fata morgana can have shown the simple Nazca Indians such complex runways and geometrical forms? I spent a long time in Nazca, and have observed it at every time of day – and never in my whole time there did I see the remotest suggestion of a mirage. Neither did any of the pilots I asked.

Or has my fellow countryman, the Swiss Professor Henri Stierlin, perhaps found the Ariadne thread that will lead us out of the Nazca labyrinth? Stierlin interpreted the Nazca lines as 'the remaining traces of gigantic weavings'.[19] This extraordinary assumption is based on the fact that the Nazca Indians were excellent weavers. Nazca weavings of wonderful colours have been found in countless graves and caverns of the region. Many of these textiles have no joins and are actually made from *one single thread*, which can be several kilometres long. One of these marvellous weavings was discovered in a cave near Paracas. It is 28 metres long, 6 metres wide, and its threads total some 50 kilometres in length.

The pre-Columbian Indians knew neither wheel nor hub, therefore they cannot have had reel, bobbin or axle for a spinning wheel. So how, asked Stierlin, the ever-practical Swiss, were the endless threads arranged without the whole thing becoming a huge tangle of knots? Nazca seemed to offer the perfect answer: they were laid out on the flat ground. Thus the long and ordered lines are the traces left behind by gigantic weavings.

I have tried to imagine this in practical terms: thousands of Indians shuffling along in single file in a straight line behind one another. In their hands they hold coloured threads which, on command, they lay down on the dust and dirt of the ground, then pick up again and continue on. The industrious weavers must have had the pattern very clearly in their heads, for no paper or papyrus patterns or drafts exist. Now woven textiles always consist of two directions, warp and weft, so the human columns in one direction must have been crossed by others. The threads of varying colour would then have to have been pulled back and forth (to the accompaniment of chanting perhaps), for the patterns always involve a constant alternation of colours. At the points where 40 lines crossed, there must have been an almighty cat's cradle!

So where then are the footprints of this busy army of weavers? Where are the tracks upon which the finished weavings were then transported? And how does Stierlin's theory explain all the drawings on cliff faces? How does it explain the straight-as-a-ruler lines that carry on over valley and mountain for up to 23 kilometres? How does it help us understand the zigzag and other lines that pass under the runways?

I'm pleased that so many brains are working overtime to solve the Nazca riddle; every new idea is to be welcomed – as long as people don't dress up their unfounded ideas as 'scientific solutions'.

Even behind the former Iron Curtain, scientists have been losing sleep over the Nazca riddle. Dr Zoltan Zelko, a mathematician from Budapest, spent years scratching his head over the phenomenon. At last – eureka! – the lightning stroke of illumination hit him: 'The lines are a map corresponding to the 800-kilometre-long, 100-kilometre-wide area of Lake Titicaca!'[20] Dear me, how on earth did he come up with that?

Around Lake Titicaca lie about 40 ruins from Inca and pre-Inca times. If one draws imaginary lines linking these ruins with certain points of high ground in the Titicaca basin, then, if Dr Zelko is to be believed, the Nazca system appears. Really? The good doctor sees this network of lines as a system for passing messages:

> News could be passed on with light signals, by means of reflecting sheets of gold or silver, or at night by fire signals. These signals were probably necessary to direct those working below in the valley and to warn them of any impending attacks.[21]

So far so bad. Between Lake Titicaca and the Nazca plain rise mighty mountain ranges, 5,000–6,000 metres high. The signals from Titicaca wouldn't have got very far! And any potential attackers threatening the Nazca Indians could not possibly have been seen by the tribes far off at Lake Titicaca. This Bolivian lake lies at an altitude of 4,000 metres – at the other end of the world as far as Nazca is concerned.

Somewhat more elevated still is the view of Siegfried Waxmann. He considers the lines of Nazca to be a 'cultural atlas of the history of humanity'.[22]

There are as many solutions as hairs on your head – if you have any left after all this! Wolf Galicki from Canada sees in the cat's cradle of

Nazca clear 'signals of an extraterrestrial intelligence'. Oh yes, and 'this is the only perspective which can enable us to understand the immense planning and incomprehensible effort that went into it.'[23]

A prehistoric Olympia?

I'll come back to earth for a minute. With his two legs firmly planted on the ground, the Munich patent lawyer Georg A von Breunig sees the scrape pictures as a pre-Inca sports field. In honour of particular gods, or as part of ritual competitions, he thinks that Indian runners sprinted along the lines and figures.[24,25] The German 'television professor', Hoimar von Ditfurth, tried – and why not? – to support this idea on screen and subsequently to immortalize it in a serious magazine.[26] At the places where the track curved, Ditfurth propounded, there ought to be greater amounts of stones and sand than where it ran along the straight. So he had measurements carried out – at two curves – which gave him the result he was looking for.

On this plain, that extends for more than 1,000 square kilometres, such hypothetical runners would have vanished from the sight of even the very best eyes. No referee would have been able to make out which figure a runner was curving around, for the drawings can be recognized only from the air. Oh yes, and I suppose the drinking water for refreshing the exhausted runners and worn-out watchers would have been on tap from the underground puquios. Well, nothing's impossible, not even the ideas of Mr Breunig. But they still do not explain the runways in the mountains, or the patterns *under* the runways. In addition, the TV programme supporting Breunig's hypothesis was 'economical' with the truth. It did not show any of the many Nazca figures on the very edge of cliffs – a subject I will return to later. No one could sprint along these. The programme carefully avoided showing any of them, for the theory would then, to say the least, have been undermined!

And what about Maria Reiche's calendar theory?

Gerald Hawkins, Professor of Astronomy at the Smithsonian Astrophysical Observatory in Cambridge, Massachusetts, took a trip to Nazca with a few colleagues. In their luggage they had the most up-to-date measuring equipment and a computer holding information about all the main constellations. The computer program also contained a time chart upon which the positions of the constellations over the last 6,900 years could be called up. After they had taken measurements in the region for several weeks, the computer printed out some devastating results. Professor Hawkins: 'No, the Nazca lines are not orientated to the stars – we were disappointed, but had to relinquish the theory of an astronomical calendar.'[27]

In spite of this clear, scientific result, one can still find specialist literature that states it to be a proven fact that the lines and scrape drawings of Nazca combine to form a gigantic astronomical calendar. Of course it must be disappointing for Maria Reiche to see a theory she had fought for all her life overthrown in the twinkling of an eye by a computer. Nevertheless, her ground-breaking achievement – the measuring and cataloguing of Nazca – remains.

So this Nazca seems to defy all logic. One theory after another bites the dust. Is there no solution that could convince everyone?

The American Jim Woodman took a practical path of investigation. He had a triangular hot-air balloon made from fine Peruvian cotton. This flying contraption was christened Kondor. Its basket, 2.5 metres long by 1.5 metre high, was woven by Aymara Indians from far-off Lake Titicaca using lightweight reeds. The first test flight took place near Cahuachi, once the chief city of the Nazca Indians: a fire was lit and hot air conducted into the balloon. Jim Woodman and Julian Nott clambered into the basket. Kondor slowly rose into the air – then the basket tipped and the two travellers fell out. But, free of their weight, the balloon took off and floated away gently like a child's balloon. After a few kilometres Kondor landed somewhere on the desert plateau.[28]

The unmanned balloon flight gave Jim Woodman a new idea. In Peru the sun shines nearly every day, and the Nazca region is particularly hot. How about a black balloon of lightweight material, which would heat up by itself during the course of the day? Perhaps the Incas gave their dead some kind of aerial burial, or their rulers paddled about in the air and looked down on the scrape drawings from above?

However natural and reasonable Jim Woodman's ideas were, they still don't solve the riddle of Nazca. For one thing, the Incas, the 'Sons of the Sun', have nothing to do with it. The Nazca trails are far older. For another, we do not know if any tribes knew about balloon flight. And if it was known about in Nazca then why was it not known elsewhere? And why would an invention of such practical use have been consigned to oblivion and forgotten? The later Incas certainly did not fly in balloons. Even the idea that the Nazca Indians sent the bodies of their dead 'up to the sun' doesn't get us any further. The balloons would have landed somewhere eventually, or their baskets would have crashed into the mountains. And anyway, since when have hot-air balloons needed runways for setting off or landing? Nor does the balloon theory tell us any more about the zigzag lines *under* the runways. Nor does it explain what measuring techniques the Nazca people employed for creating their giant figures and drawings.

More practical approaches

In 1977 the resident archaeologist in Nazca, Josué Lancho, began an experiment. The idea actually came from a BBC journalist. Would it still be possible to create a Nazca marking using only modest equipment? Josué Lancho asked 30 young Indians to help him. Using three wooden stakes and strings they managed, in less than three days, to scratch a narrow, straight line of 150 metres in the pampa surface.[29] Now straight lines don't pose a measuring problem; and in fact isolated remains of wooden stakes have been found on the desert surface of Nazca. Professor Anthony Aveni and a few volunteers from the organisation Earthwatch then tried to make the first curve of a spiral. The stones were scraped away from the surface with hands and feet and gathered together in small piles. The curve was made simply by laying out strings by eye. The result was a small, imperfect circle roughly 3 metres in diameter.

Both experiments proved that *narrow* lines – that is, ones which are no more than a metre broad – are fairly easy to make. But what about the large figures – the spider, the monkey, the humming bird? What about the broad and kilometre-long runways and trapezoids?

In the cartographic department of the Institute for Technology and Economics in Dresden, an amazing project is currently in progress, led by Professors Gunter Reppchen and Bernd Teichert. They are collating all the figures and lines of Nazca in a large-scale, digital relief model. Dresden is after all the birthplace of Maria Reiche, so it is only right that her work should be carried on by the local university. After a seminar at the Swiss Institute of Technology in Zurich on 10 October 1996, the question of the amount of land cleared of stones was raised. How many cubic centimetres of stones had been carried away by the Nazca Indians? Professor Reppchen believed it must have been in the region of 10,000 cubic metres. I estimate it must have been far more because, besides the runways, one must take into account the mountain summits in the Nazca region that had to be levelled in order to make them. Compared with such a scale of operations, the two tiny experiments carried out in Nazca seem pretty insignificant.

The 102 books, brochures and articles which are my source material on Nazca, are riddled with repetitions and claptrap, as well as intentional distortions and falsehoods. To mention all of them would be not only boring but an imposition on my readers. Why should *my* readers want to hear that a university lecturer reported to *his* readers that, in my first book, *Chariots of the Gods?*, I failed to refer to the Frenchmen Louis Pauwels and Jacques Bergier as my source?[30] Or that the drawings of Nazca were not 'burned into the hard rock with extraterrestrial lasers', nor 'plastered on with a mysterious substance from another world', as I am apparently meant to have informed my readers. No such nonsense is to be found in my books, any more than the following garbage:

According to von Däniken's favoured hypothesis, we are to assume (unproven) the existence of intelligent, extraterrestrial life, then to suppose that these extraterrestrials visited the earth in a distant past (unproven and highly improbable), and finally to conclude that these extraterrestrials needed to build strange runways (very hard to believe). After all this, apparently, for their further entertainment, they instructed the local inhabitants to draw gigantic pictures of birds, spiders, monkeys and snakes in the ground.[31]

This is the sort of way in which scientific literature seeks to enlighten the youth of today and the media. It's not worth replying. Scientific

TV programmes are also concocted from such old wives' tales, then distributed world-wide and shown to young people in schools. I can't be bothered to take the time to respond to such distortions. But how can opinion be altered? Surely only through conclusive pictures and compelling arguments!

An assertion is an unproven assumption. I make the following assertions:

1 In the mountains of Nazca there is a large rectangle of scraped earth, in which two circles have been placed. Inside the circles are two more superimposed rectangles, and at the centre is a 'crown' of radiating lines.

2 This mysterious pattern is connected to two additional geometrical forms: to the right and left, diagonally behind them, are further circles with geometrical subdivisions. One can imagine a gigantic sail: in the centre foreground is the main segment, with the 'swivel-sail' behind.

3 On a cliff-edge in the Nazca region there lies a huge 'chessboard' design, composed of more than 1,000 points and stripes – a filigree work of great precision.

4 In the mountains around Nazca there are figures of up to 40 metres in height, some of which have been discovered only very recently. They wear 'helmets', from which there often sprout what look like giant antennae.

5 There are other regions of the earth besides Peru where people have made scrape drawings. Signs for the gods.

6 In Chile, at a height of 2,400 metres, a runway track has been discovered. It is so old that geological formations have partially covered it over the last few thousand years.

7 One will not be able to discover a unifying system for the Nazca region. Everything found there arose at different times, and was made by Indian tribes with differing perspectives and ideas.

In the following chapter I will try to provide proof for my assertions.

Notes

1 Bray Warwick, 'Under the skin of Nazca', *Nature*, vol. 358, 2 July 1992.

2 'Das Alter der Nazca-Scharrbilder', *Neue Zürcher Zeitung*, 2 September 1992.

3 Anthony F Aveni and Helaine Silverman, 'Between the Lines. Reading the Nazca Markings as Rituals Writ Large', *The Sciences*, New York Academy of Sciences, July/August 1991.

4 Helaine Silverman, 'Beyond the Pampa: The Geoglyphs in the Valleys of Nazca', *National Geographic Research and Exploration*, 1990, pp. 435–56.

5 Aldon J Mason, *Das alte Peru, Eine indianische Hochkultur*, Zurich, 1957.

6 Simone Waisbard, 'Nazca – Zeichen in der Wüste', *Die letzten Geheimnisse unserer Welt*, Stuttgart, 1977.

7 Robert L Forward, 'Ad Astra!', *Journal of the British Interplanetary Society*, vol. 49, 1996, pp. 23–32.

8 Gregory L Matloff, 'Robosloth – a slow interstellar Thin-Film Robot', *Journal of the British Interplanetary Society*, vol. 49, 1996, pp. 33–6.

9 Waisbard, op. cit.

10 Ibid.

11 Michael D Coe (ed.), *Die Nazca Scharrbilder*, Munich, 1986.

12 Albrecht Kottmann, *Uralte Verbindungen zwischen Mittelmeer und Amerika. Gleiche Maßeinheiten beidseits des Atlantiks*, Stuttgart, 1988.

13 Evan Hadingham, *Lines to the Mountain Gods*, London, 1987.

14 William H Isbell, 'Die Bodenzeichnungen Altperus', *Spektrum der Wissenschaft*, December 1978.

15 Helmut Tributsch, *Das Rätsel der Götter – Fata Morgana*, Frankfurt/Main, 1983.

16 Ibid.

17 Dileep Kumar Kanjilal, *Vimana in Ancient India (Aeroplanes or Flying Machines in Ancient India)*, trans. Julia Zimmermann, Bonn, 1991.

18 Lutz Gentes, *Die Wirklichkeit der Götter. Raumfahrt im frühen Indien*, Munich/Essen, 1996.

19 Henri Stierlin, *Nazca, la clef du mystère*, Paris, 1982.

20 'Ist das Liniensystem in der Nazca-Ebene eine Landkarte?', *Voralberger Nachrichten*, Bregenz, 16 May 1981.

21 Ibid.

22 Siegfried Waxmann, *Unsere Lehrmeister aus dem Kosmos*, Ebersbach, 1982.

23 Wolf Galicki, *The Nazca Desert 'Chart'*, Denman Island, BC, 1978.

24 Georg A von Breunig, 'Nazca: A pre-Columbian Olympian Site?', *Intercienca,* vol. 5, no. 4, 1980.

25 Georg A von Breunig, *Nazca, A Gigantic Sports Arena? A New Approach for Explaining the Origin of the Desert Markings in the Basin of Rio Grande in Southern Peru*, University of Northern Colorado, Museum of Antropology, nd.

26 Hoimar von Ditfurth, 'Warum der Mensch zum Renner wurde', *Geo*, no. 12, December 1981.

27 Gerald H Hawkins, 'Die Bodenzeichnungen Altperus', *Spektrum der Wissenschaft*, December 1978.

28 Jim Woodman, *Nazca*, Munich, 1977.

29 Tony Morrison, *Das Geheimnis der Linien von Nazca*, Basel and Stuttgart, 1987.

30 Kenneth L Feder, *Frauds, Myths and Mysteries. Science and Pseudoscience in Archaeology*, Central Connecticut State University, nd.

31 Ibid.

ARGUMENTS FOR THE IMPOSSIBLE

4

First make yourself unpopular,
then people will take you seriously.
KONRAD ADENAUER, 1876–1967

'Eduardo,' I said to the chief pilot of Aero Condor, 'I know the plain of Nazca pretty well by now. Let's do something different. I'd like to go in larger and larger circles each day. From Nazca to the mountains, but so that I have the chance to see every valley, hill and cliff face.'

That was in the autumn of 1995.

Eduardo grinned: 'That will take a while. And it'll cost you!'

'Can't help that. Each day I'll be at the airstrip at 6.30 in the morning, and again at close to 5 o'clock in the afternoon. We'll take out the door on the co-pilot's side so that I've got a clear view.'

So that's what we did. I hung three cameras with different lenses round my neck, crammed my pockets full of film and squatted, leaning forward, on the co-pilot's seat. I put my right foot outside the cabin on a small ledge that was really meant as a step for passengers entering the plane. I put the safety belt round my hips, and also had a small rope strung across my shoulders. With these safety measures in place we took off – day after day.

Immediately after our first take-off, Eduardo ascended in a spiral to 1,300 metres above Nazca's little airfield.

'I'd like to show you something that we only recently discovered!' bawled out Eduardo. Then he headed for the summit of an arid-looking slope.

'There! Do you see it?'

At first I saw nothing. The slope was brown and rocky, the same monotonous colour everywhere. But when we flew over for a second time I noticed rectangular designs on the upper slope, then figures like robots with hoods, from which ribbon-like strips dangled down.[74] Then finally I saw the outline of a 20-metre-high creature, hard to recognize and – since it was brown on brown – impossible to photograph. The head was filled by two giant, round eyes. The forehead came to a point at the top, and from the skull grew several tentacle-like 'growths' which were larger than its whole body. The body itself was delicately built. Thin little legs and arms protruded from a torso that was only twice as big as the head. But this body was also equipped with wavy tentacles on both sides.

'What's this mountain called?' I asked.

'Doesn't have a name!' he shouted in my ear. We call it Cerro de los Astronautas (Summit of the Astronauts)!'

This is doubtless not a name that the scientists will be happy to adopt!

In 1983, on a lower slope, a very similar figure was discovered. In the scientific literature it has been called a 'mystical being with carefully drawn tentacles'.[1] The specialists regard it as a fabulous being or 'water divinity'. (The precise location for those who would like to see it for themselves is: longitude: 14°, 42', 26"; latitude: 75°, 6', 38".)

In Nazca there is another figure generally referred to as 'el Astronauta'. It adorns the sheer slope of a hill at the southern end of the Pampa de San José, and is 29 metres high.[75] Its skull is dominated by two round eyes, the body's proportions are normal and the feet seem to be wearing ungainly shoes. The arms are interesting: one points to the heavens, the other to the earth. Is it telling us something about the connection between earth and the heavens? The figure is enclosed by two vertical lines. There must originally have been other figures on this slope – you can just make out the traces of their outlines. And the whole image has a startling three-dimensional effect when the sun is in a certain position, becoming visible from below as though emerging from the mountain. On a hilltop there is a sequence of smaller images – various animals lined up one behind the other as though in a comic; also creatures with long, dinosaur-like tails. Friends of the Cabrera collection, I'd say! Unfortunately the photos of this came out badly –

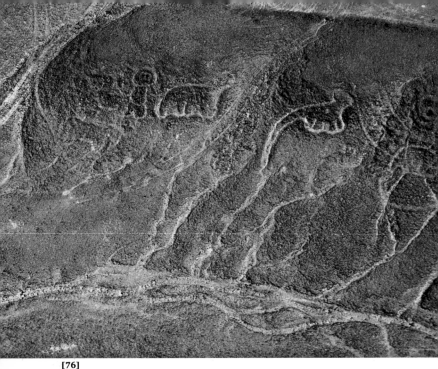

[76]

I'm still cross with myself for not asking Eduardo to turn round so that I could get some more shots. The photo [76] printed here shows only a part of this 'art gallery'.

Shining figures

The pictures of the 'antennae-beings' are a good deal better. A 20-metre-high figure[77] waves from the bottom of a slope. It wears a hat-like thing with a wide brim and from this head-adornment feelers extend upwards. The arms are spread wide as though the figure is dancing, and in each hand the creature holds something – it is not clear what. There are several such figures.

Particularly impressive and thought-provoking is an image over 25 metres high and about 20 metres broad.[78] It is one which I have not found mentioned anywhere in the literature on Nazca. On the left is a mystical looking creature – whatever mystical means – with a triangular head, big round eyes and a small round mouth. The head is

[77]

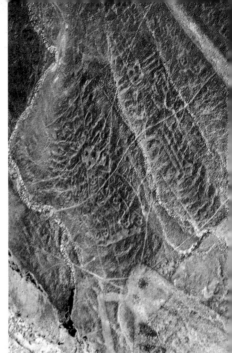

[78]

[79]

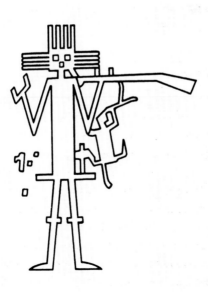

111

surrounded by a wreath of zigzag lines that look like flower petals or stylized feathers. From its shoulders dangle broad tentacles the length of its body, furnished at the ends with circles or small skulls. On the right of this figure is another one, looking like a robot. Nine straight lines protrude from its head in three different directions. The lower body spreads out like a dress or a sail. Right next to this creature is the head of a child, and above it and only just visible is another 'antennae-being'.

This picture ought to be held in high regard by all Nazca theoreticians. Why? Because a 'copy' of it can be seen in the north of Chile on an arid mountain slope above the desert of Taratacar. It was discovered by the Chilean airforce general, Eduardo Jensen. The figure is called the 'Giant of Cerro Unitas', and is all of 121 metres high. The Taratacar region is part of the great desert of Atacama. Unfortunately the place is also the site of the Chilean airforce's practice target range, so the giant figure is continually bombarded, even used as a target. Just like his 'twin' in Nazca, the head of the 'Giant of Cerro Unitas' is equipped with 'antennae'. The body of the Chilean figure is rectangular too, and its lower end is closed off by a horizontal 'cross-beam'. In both figures the arms are bent at an angle and end in crude, pincer-like tongs.[79] The only difference is that the Chilean copy has a small monkey at its right arm, though the Nazca twin may also originally have had one too.

How did this come about? It ought to give us pause for thought, for Nazca and the target range of Taratacar are separated by a distance of 1,300 air kilometres.

Many figures closely resembling those on the mountain slopes can be found in the form of Nazca pottery. The 1,000-dollar question about whether the pottery or the figures came first is not an easy one to answer. I believe the figures on the mountains came first, because they would have been constantly visible to the Indians, staring down at them from the heights. This is *not* the case with the figures on the surface of the desert – which can only be seen by flying over them. Now there are, it has to be said, Nazca ceramics which show similar – though not identical – motifs to those on the desert surface. So what came first, the ceramics or the scrape drawing? If the ceramics came first, we have to ask how the Indians managed to enlarge their designs to such gargantuan proportions. And if the scrape drawings were there

[80]

[81]

[82]

113

first, where did the Indians stand so as to be able to see them clearly enough to transfer the designs to their pottery? The same is true for their textiles.

Most of the figures on the mountain walls are equipped with 'antennae', 'tentacles' or wreaths of rays.[80, 81] But those on the pampa are not. Were the 'ray-wreathed' figures therefore depictions of particularly great and mysterious individuals? Beings who existed at a *higher level* than that of ordinary people? Gods?

This suspicion is confirmed by the excavations at Sican, north of Lima in the Lambayeque region (near Batan Grande). Peruvian and Japanese archaeologists worked there for 16 years, until their efforts were crowned by a phenomenal discovery. In 1991, amazing graves were found at a depth of 10 metres, containing textiles and about 50 kilos of precious stones and metals, among them the golden mask of the 'God of Sican'.[82] The word 'Sican' comes from the ancient language of the Muchiks, also called the Mochica in Colombia and Ecuador, and means Temple of the Moon. In either hand the figure holds strange 'ceremonial staffs', also sometimes interpreted as 'sceptres'. From its head protrude four 'antennae' on each side. Remind you of anything?

Visible only to the gods!

The similarity between depictions found at some distance apart from each other can hardly be denied. They cannot just be water gods or mountain gods.

How could they be? What do the 'ray-figures' of Nazca or 'el Astronauta' on the top of a hill have to do with water? The mountain gods dreamed up by archaeology are also unconvincing. If they are 'mountain gods' then surely they should demonstrate some intrinsic connection with the mountains – but I fail to see how one can interpret them in that way! The robot of Taratacar in northern Chile adorns a desert mountain slope. No water to be a god of! And he can't be thought of as a mountain god – any more than the Pintados in the Atacama desert can. That is also in Chile, north-west of Antofagasta near the little town of San Pedro de Atacama. Just where the priest

Le Paige built his museum. (He was the one, you may remember, who said he had found graves containing the skeletons of extraterrestrials.)

That region could almost be on Mars: it is completely dried up, with not a drop of water for miles. The mountain slopes there are engraved with curious earth drawings, made in the same way as those at Nazca. But there are no runways or narrow straight lines. And they were obviously not done just to pass the time. For the Indians who lived there in a cauldron of heat, these signs – for example, the two rectangles with an arrow beside them – must have been some kind of message. Each side of the two rectangles is formed by four circles. From the lower rectangle a double arrow points downwards.[83] There is no water there, nor an underground water course. And then there is the 'flying god with the wheel', which consists of two triangles, in the upper of which are two eyes and a large mouth. On its right and left sides spread two wings, and over the whole image floats a wheel, sub-divided into several segments.[84] And there are other forms which are reminiscent of hieroglyphics: in the upper line are two symbols, in the next line eight, and in the last line a further two. To the right again

[83]

are a large circle and various 'antennae-people'.[85, 86] And these aren't little drawings such as you find in cave paintings, but up to 20 metres high on the slope of a mountain, pointing in the direction of the sky.

Even more remarkable is the 'ladder with an arrow'.[87] It starts with a broad horizontal stroke scraped away from the hill, which is crossed by a vertical ladder whose lower end becomes an arrow. The whole image is surrounded by indefinable figures, an animal with a long neck and various rectangular surfaces.

These Pintados in the Chilean desert of Atacama are as incomprehensible as the drawings on the Nazca pampa. Those at Nazca at least represent more or less identifiable things such as birds, fish, a spider or a monkey, while the Pintados show us a strange kind of geometry. For example, a vertical line runs for 25 metres towards the summit of the highest point. At the top the line is crowned with a circle.[88]

There are also cliff drawings in the region, such as a figure without arms and with rays emanating from its head, surrounded by

[87]

animals.[89] I know of very similar drawings tens of thousands of kilometres away – those of the Aborigines in Australia. There are masses of them in the Kimberley mountains. Just as there, one can see cliff drawings in the Atacama desert which apparently depict boats. In each 'boat' can be seen the rudimentary outlines of two human forms. And – still in the Atacama desert – there are gods (if that's what they are) with 'ceremonial staffs' or 'sceptres', similar to the god of Sican in Peru.

It is not a good idea to study Nazca in isolation from other places. Apart from Chile, far to the south of Nazca (and even in Chile the Atacama desert is not the only example), there are other sites where signs pointing to the heavens can be found. Let me cite three further places that would be of interest to Nazca investigators if they wish to broaden their horizons.

On the desert floor of Majes and Sihuas in the Peruvian province of Arequipa are gigantic scrape drawings pointing towards the sky.

[88]   [89]

From the south-Peruvian town of Mollendo down to the deserts and mountains of the Chilean province of Antofagasta lie great scrape drawings. All done for the eyes of the gods. And not only in the interior of the country, but on the coast as well.

In Chile, in the Cordillera de Chicauma, a few kilometres from Lampa, but at a height of 2,400 metres, 140 signs were found which had *not* been scraped out of the ground. Pointing to the heavens, they consist of little walls and piles of stones. Among them is a runway which, beyond doubt, is at least as old as the oldest runway at Nazca. However old that is. Why do I think that? Because rock formations have grown *over* it! The picture[90] which was given to me by the Chilean journalist Jaime Bascur is not of very good quality, yet good enough to make out the salient details. So why *must* it be a 'runway'? Because it begins and ends abruptly. It can't be a road from A to B; and if anyone thinks it's something to do with mountain gods, they're beyond help as far as I can see.

[90]

So was the laying down of signs pointing to heaven confined to people south of Nazca? Not at all! The broad lava fields in the Mexican Sonora desert are adorned with similar markings.

Further north, at the Mexican-Californian border, lies the desert landscape of Macahui. Some scrub and bushes grow here, which is why the mystery of Macahui was not immediately seen from the air. The region stretches away to the north of the road running between Tijuana and Mexicali. There, in an area of 400 square kilometres, signs were discovered which had been scratched into the ground, and which no one has yet been able to explain. One part consists of circles – one after another as far as the eye can see. Then there are rectangles, half-moons, wheels with several compartments, interwoven rings and drop-like forms. The dimensions of individual signs are anything up to

[91]

[92]

40 metres. Unlike Nazca, there are no pictures of animals or humans – at least not on the Mexican side of the border. Let me quickly warn any enthusiasts who might like to go there and take pictures that this region lies on *both sides* of the border, and you certainly need permission to visit the US side. And there are poisonous snakes under every stone!

Further north, not far from the little town of Blythe by the Colorado River, there are figures of people and animals, up to 100 metres in height, which can be seen only from the air.[91, 92] These have been scraped out of the ground like the Nazca figures.

In Arizona, near Sacaton, there is a human figure 46 metres long.

And further north, from the Rocky Mountains to the Appalachians, there are roughly 5,000! 'picture-hills', called Indian Mounds. These depict birds, bears, snakes and lizards, and often contained the graves of great chieftains. Although we know who made these particular pictures, it is worth noting that the motifs can be seen properly only from the air.

A compelling insight

No one can dispute that all over America – North, Central and South – many Indian communities carried on the practice or cult of giant earth drawings. Equally indisputable is the fact that most of these images can be seen only from the air. How can people go on talking about 'water and mountain gods' when faced with pictures such as the ones reproduced in this book? Shouldn't scientific research broaden its scope beyond the confined horizons of Nazca? Normal scientific method involves taking into account all possible aspects of a problem and looking for a common factor that can make sense of it. In the case of Nazca this kind of procedure has obviously been thrown to the winds. Anyone who ever saw the inside of a university is permitted to regard himself as an expert in the matter. If he has an academic title as well, so much the better.

What *is* the common factor of almost all the earth drawings? *That they can be seen properly only from the air.* They lie in all sorts of different places and regions – in deserts, on mountain slopes, at heights of 2,400 metres, on grassy plains (like the Indian Mounds) or on gravel surfaces. It doesn't actually matter where they are, the fact remains that the air is the only place to see them from. Jim Woodman's balloon theory was tried out at Nazca. Why not in Chile or Mexico as well? There are giant scrape drawings there too – but no runways.

Professor Aveni's theory relies on the behaviour of Indians in Cuzco *nowadays*. Were the same people active in Mexico's Sonora desert? The archaeologist Simone Waisbard thinks Nazca's 'picture book' existed to 'determine the amount of rainfall'. And what about the 'Giant of Cerro Unitas' in Chile? Were his antennae perhaps useful for assessing rainfall? What rainfall? It doesn't rain in the desert, neither in winter nor summer. The rectangles at Nazca were, apparently, 'ceremonial places'. And those on the sloping mountain walls near San Pedro de Atacama? There are also scraped rectangles there, but it can hardly have been a suitable gathering place for pious pilgrims because of the angle of the slope.[93] And what about Professor Isbell's idea of 'occupational therapy'? Was that true, too, for the Mexican Indians in the desert landscape of Macahui? And how

[93]

about Professor Tributsch's fata morgana? It isn't even right for Nazca, let alone the Atacama desert.

So it goes on – a catalogue of academic garbage. Nothing can be proved yet everyone thinks his own theory is proven. And no one looks further than the backyard of Nazca. Nazca alone is already a mixed salad with all sorts of ingredients, in which every well-intentioned opinion is contradicted by other facts. Woodman's hot-air balloons do not need runways; the narrow lines are not an astronomical calendar; the runways cannot have anything to do with mountain gods; and the Indian athletes who supposedly ran along the lines of the figures and shapes could not have done so on mountain slopes.

Only one single fact holds good: the signs are properly recognizable only from the air. And by the way, there are also such signs in England, at Lake Aral near Ustjurt and in the Saudi-Arabian desert.[2]

Since this is the common, unifying factor, we must assume that our forefathers all over the globe at least *believed* that someone 'up there' would see their pictures. Contrary to the accusation sometimes levelled at me that I think ancient people were not particularly intelligent, I would say they were actually very clued-up indeed. They certainly weren't so stupid as lay down enormous markings on the ground for generation after generation with no hope of them being seen by some gods or other. Which gods? All the suggestions that rise up out of the murk and mist of psychology are useless, since they are valid only within certain limited parameters. Whoever wants to can look for mountain gods in Nazca – but not, for heaven's sake, in the Sonora desert! Those who think the Nazca Indians were so dumb that they laid down gigantic lines for the sake of water gods can hang on to this theory if they like – but it cannot be produced like a rabbit from a magician's hat to explain the 'Giant of Cerro Unitas', for that is really beyond the bounds of possibility.

So who first came upon the idea of looking for 'flying gods' in the firmament? This theme is obviously universal – every culture has its own versions. But that is not enough of an explanation, for these 'heavenly gods' didn't just spring from some deluded imagination. These gods were once real. Whoever categorically dismisses this proposition has no clue about ancient Indian literature,[3,4] knows nothing of the sayings of the anti-deluriam prophet Enoch,[5] and has never heard of the *Kebra Negest*.[6] In this, in the book of the 'Glory of Kings', are described various flights which King Solomon took – including mention of the speed at which the king travelled. Let me quote:

> The king and all who obeyed his command, *flew upon the chariot* without illness or suffering, without hunger or thirst, without sweat or tiring. *In one day they completed a journey of three months* ... besides various other chariots, he [Solomon] also gave her [the queen of Sheba] one which *flew through the air*, which he had prepared in accordance with the wisdom with which God had endowed him [my italics]

And further on:

> Long time ago the people of the land of Egypt passed through this place, riding upon a chariot like the angels, and quicker than the eagle in the sky.

And for anyone who still wants to dispute prehistoric flight, let me slip in two examples from Indian literature:

> So the king [Rumanvat] sat down with his harem servants, his wives and his dignitaries *in the heavenly chariot. They reached the expanses of the firmament and followed the route of the winds. The heavenly chariot flew round the globe, over the oceans* and was then steered in the direction of the town of Avantis, where a festival was taking place. After this short pause in their journey, the king set off once more in front of countless people who had gathered to marvel at this heavenly chariot [my italics][7]

> Arjuna wished for Indra's heavenly chariot to reach him. And with Matali the chariot suddenly arrived in a glitter of lights, banishing darkness from the air and illuminating the clouds, filling everywhere with a noise like thunder ...[8]

No one can tell me that this was all psychologically explainable wishful-thinking, or the poetic licence of biographers wanting to glorify their rulers. Claptrap! I know the ancient texts with their precise descriptions,

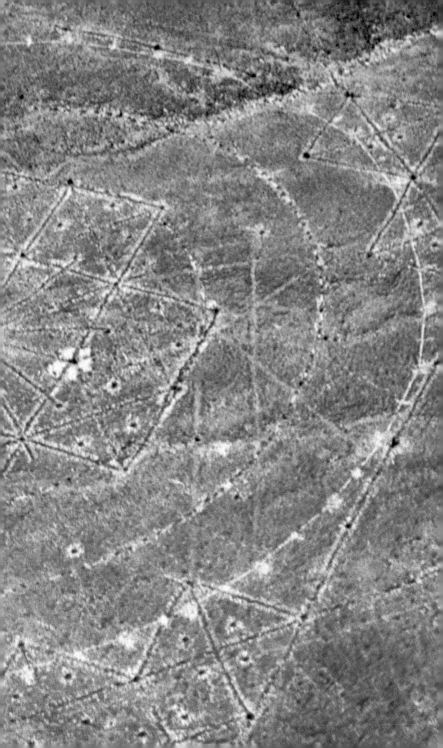

in which the various metal alloys used, as well as weapons systems, are listed exactly.[9] I have long since lost the habit of seeing one thing when I read another.

Whenever people fly they need, at least, primitive instruments or simple landing orientations. Where might these be found in Nazca?

The phenomenal discovery!

The first time I saw the shape below me I thought I was seeing things – an optical illusion of some kind. I asked the pilot Eduardo to fly over it again … and again and again. And as the plane climbed up to 800 metres, I saw the second phenomenon, linked to the first. As well as the usual photos, I took two with an instant-picture camera. Later, sitting in the shade with a cool drink, I stared at the pictures – not yet dreaming that the next day's flight would throw up two even greater surprises.

First I saw a large circle on whose circumference were more than 60 points. Then I perceived within this first circle a second with countless smaller points on its circumference. In the middle were two superimposed rectangles, each divided into eight squares.[94] These squares were divided by crossing lines from each corner, and in the very centre of the form lay a bundle of 16 lines radiating outwards. What was it? On the second photo I noticed that the whole geometrical pattern was enclosed by two giant squares lying diagonally one on top of the other.

My first thought was of a mandala of some kind, such as the Tibetans and Hindus use in the practice of meditation. The North American Indians have something similar, which they call sand-paintings, composed of many geometrical forms and colours. If the complicated geometrical pattern in front of me was some kind of mandala, then it had to be a modern forgery. Or perhaps a teacher had taken a class of pupils to Nazca and got them to do this for a lark. I had taken my photograph in the Palpa mountains, about 12 minutes' flight from the Nazca airstrip. The mountains there are quite arid; the region is like hell on earth. This geometrical form was so complicated

◁ [94] and large scale – approximately 500 metres in diameter – that the group of fakers must have spent an awful long time in the sweltering heat. And their foot and car tracks should have been visible. No one goes to hell with slippers on! Not even the Peruvian army – and they would have left the tracks of their vehicles. I stared at the picture again and again. There were individual lines which did not belong to the geometrical form. Later on, when I was able to compare these shots with the photographs taken with other cameras, I saw that the fainter lines belonged to the network of Nazca lines. I asked Eduardo, and other pilots too, to suggest who might have carried out this modern forgery.

'That's not modern, nor fake – it was always there!'

'Then why is it not mentioned in any of the Nazca tourist guides? I don't ever remember seeing a picture of it before,' I said doubtfully.

They told me that, firstly, the diagram was not on the plain of Nazca but in Palpa, and, secondly, no one knew how to explain it. So they kept mum.

I couldn't stop thinking about this geometrical form. The next day we flew back there. Only then, from a greater height, did I notice that the first 'mandala' was connected with a second, and then – from a still greater height – with a third.[95, 96] It was extraordinary! I could forget any ideas of a modern forgery – the proportions of the whole thing were enough to discount that possibility. All three forms together spread over more than a kilometre. In addition – and that made the whole thing still more mysterious – there was a geological cleft running through the middle of the pattern. It began at a corner of the inner rectangle, broadened out, then passed through the two circles and out beyond the enclosing square frame. The crazy thing was that the circumference points and lines passed over the cleft, as if it had been of no importance to the creator of the pattern.

Extending on the form's left-hand side, the base line of the great square became the centre of a double circle. The same thing was repeated on the right-hand side, where there were two more large rings, one lying inside the other. From the centre ran straight lines in the four directions of the compass. From a great height the three diagrams presented a phenomenal picture: in the foreground the giant main circle framed by the two squares, then right and left the two connected rings. And everything connected by lines to everything else. **[95]** ▷

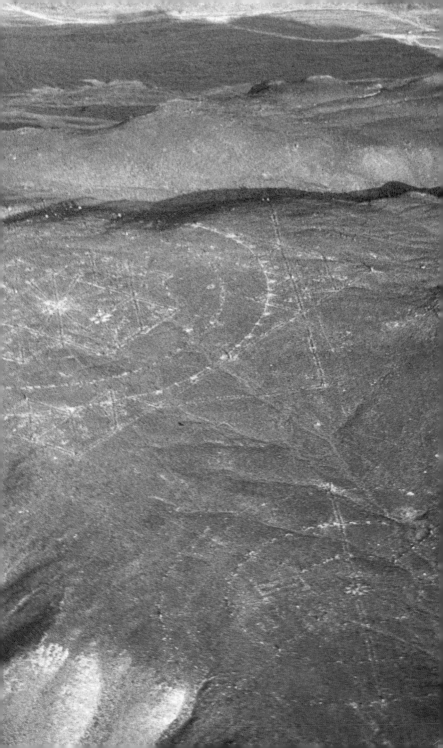

If a thick stroke were to be drawn over the whole thing, the image of a gigantic arrow would emerge.

We circled for a long time and at different altitudes over this vast diagram, which had, in recent times at least, been ignored by all previous observers. I puzzled and racked my brain as to its purpose. A geometrical pattern in the form of an arrow? Were there yet stranger things to be discovered? Eduardo shook his head. Sometimes, he said, you saw things here that later disappeared. It depended on the angle of the light and the time of day. I asked him to fly over the next valleys and to keep following a thin line that led away from the diagram.

Suddenly I cried out: 'Stop!', realizing at the same time how impossible my order was – we were after all in an aeroplane. I had glimpsed something, though only for a fraction of a second.

'What was it?' asked Eduardo.

'No idea,' I shouted back. But it was something. I saw strange points glinting. Let's go back.'

Eduardo flew round while I strained my eyes to see what was below. Because of the missing door I had a better view than my pilot. After circling again I was very disappointed – I had seen nothing more, yet was absolutely certain that there was something unusual below. At the third flight round, this time at 500 metres, I began to exclaim with joy.

'Look, Eduardo, look! Unbelievable! Here, right below me!'

Eduardo tipped the plane to one side. Then he saw it too.

On the summit of a mountain lay a chessboard of white points and lines – another phenomenal discovery. It was a giant, rectangular design, also with a cleft running through it. To its left ran some narrow 'Nazca lines' in pairs. This 'chessboard' consisted of 36 lines across and 15 lengthways, arranged in dots and dashes like Morse code.[97, 98] The whole pattern lay on an uneven summit. To its right was a steep slope, and below in the valley a dried-up river bed. It suddenly struck me that neither the geometrical form nor the chessboard pattern could have been made by the same Indians who created the Nazca figures. This was something quite different. There were no scrape drawings here, no Nazca runways, no animal or human figures. And no archaeological missionary seeing this could preach about mountain gods, water gods, [96] psychological gobbledygook, mirages or occupational therapy!

134

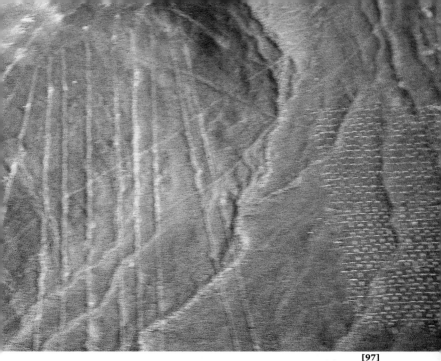

[97]

A well-founded theory

Here we have, then – for all who care to see – nothing other than geometry and mathematics. But for what purpose? One thing I realized straightaway was that both the chessboard and the gigantic geometrical form were visible only to those who knew how to fly. A non-flyer would have no chance of seeing these two patterns. Even if someone came across them by chance in the course of a crazy hike across the mountains in baking heat, he wouldn't be aware of them. But anyway, no path leads to them, and no mountain gods, however magic and mystical, would be of much use in getting there. No, these patterns were made for flyers. And every pilot knows similar patterns. Peter Belting from Aurich in Germany, himself a brilliant pilot, pointed this out to me. He explained that such patterns are called VASIS or PAPI sites. VASIS stands for Visual Approach Side Indicator System, a visual landing-approach system that shows the pilot whether he is too high, low or close to the approach corridor. The PAPI (Precision Approach [98] ▷

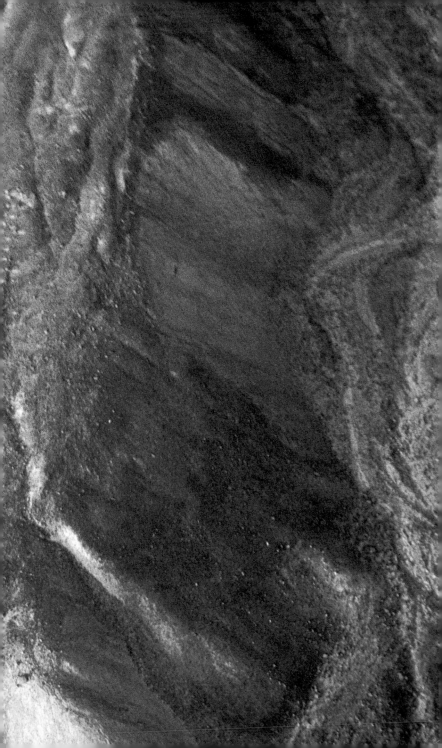

Path Indicator) site has the same function. Such landing aids consist of lights and colours. The pilot can recognize from his position in relation to the light sections how far he is from an ideal landing angle. Nowadays VASIS or PAPI sites work by means of electric light, but they can also function without it. The pattern itself, of geometrical lines or colours, can show the pilot if he needs to alter his position for landing. These aids are also used by automatic pilot systems.

Does this have anything to do with Nazca? What follows is my theory, to which I will append some 'landing aids' to help substantiate it.

The Sanskrit literature of ancient India described how there were once gigantic space cities which orbited the earth. To check this, I suggest that my critics look up the 'Drona Parva' volume of the *Mahabharata*. (Every fair-sized university library should have a copy of this work.) It was translated into English in 1888 by the then renowned Sanskrit scholar Professor Protap Chandra Roy.[10] At that time, Professor Chandra Roy could not have dreamt that such things as 'space-towns' might one day actually exist. Page 690, verse 62 of the 'Drona Parva' reads: 'Originally the brave Asuras possessed three towns in the heavens. Each of these towns was great and excellently built ... In spite of all his weaponry, Maghavat did not succeed in making any impression upon these heavenly towns ...' And on page 691, verse 50 it states: 'then the three towns in the firmament met together ...' It should be clear from this passage that some vague heaven of spiritual contentment is not meant, but rather the *firmament*, the physical heavens above us.

From these space-towns various types of aircraft, which the Indians called *vimanas*, visited the earth. One of these landed in the Nazca region. Of course it needed no *runway*, and anyway, no one would yet have made one. Why should a contingent of extraterrestrials land in the arid and inhospitable region of Nazca? Because the area is chock-full of minerals: iron, gold and silver. Drilling is still carried out there, and south-east of Nazca, intensive mining continues.[99, 100] The Marcona mine is the largest in Peru – not only for iron, but for minerals of all kinds.

Critics, including Maria Reiche, who say that the ground under the surface of Nazca is too soft to bear the weight of a heavy machine,

◁ [98]

[99]

[100]

understand nothing about space travel. The Americans no doubt worried about the same problem before the moon landing. No one knew whether the moon surface would support a spaceship as it landed – but a technological society can resolve such uncertainties.

The landing created a trapezoid surface on the ground. The trapezoid is broadest where the landing craft put down, and narrowest where the eddies of air made least impact on the ground.

From distant hills and mountains the native Indians watched the activities of the strangers with fear and astonishment. Human-like beings with golden, shimmering skins walked around, bored holes in the ground, gathered rocks and did unknown things with strange tools. Then one day there was a thunderous noise. The Indians rushed to their observation posts and saw the 'heavenly chariot' ascending into the sky.

That was the beginning of Nazca as a place of pilgrimage. It was now 'holy ground'. The gods had been there!

Yet the gods soon returned, this time with other heavenly chariots. (In the Indian Sanskrit texts, 20 different vimanas are described, with and without wheels, with and without wings, quiet, loud, etc). At one spot the gods laid a narrow, coloured tape on the ground and bent it into a zigzag line. It contained landing and take-off information for the vimanas, as on an aircraft carrier. But the inhabitants of the area couldn't have known this. Finally the gods placed huge geometric patterns on the mountain summits, which served as landing orientation, like the VASIS or PAPI sites of today. The natives would have had no clue what purpose these served. Then the gods began to dismantle things and to fly away with them. It is quite possible that the raw material the strangers needed could have been obtained from open-cast mining or scraping, rather than by boring.

All this activity may have lasted weeks or months. No one will ever know – unless of course the gods return and explain what took place there.

At last peace returned to this region. The gods had departed and taken all their equipment with them. The bravest Indians crept to the place where the strangers had been, then stood around wondering what the heavenly beings had been doing. Nothing was left apart from a few trapezoid shapes on the ground and a broad track with a snakelike line underneath it. And two or three strange rings and rectangles on a few hilltops.

The beginning of a cult

Being inquisitive, as people are, small groups kept coming back to this mystical place. They talked together and assured one another that it had really happened, that chariots of the gods had come down from the heavens. But what did the signs that the gods had left behind them mean? Could they have meant that human beings should make similar designs for the gods? Was this what the heavenly powers expected of mankind?

The priests gave the order and the people obeyed. Nazca became a place of worship. And because the number of Indians there continually increased, more and more fields had to be cultivated. This in turn required more water – and an enormous undertaking to provide it, but for the sake of the gods this was done. The Indians began to build water channels and clear large fields for planting. In all directions there arose lines and trapezoid surfaces as one tribe tried to outdo another. They all slaved away in the blessed hope that the gods would return and reward them for their dedicated service.

Years and decades passed, generations came and went. The priests observed the sky: from up there, from those distant points of light, the gods had once come. This was well known, for people now dead had seen it with their own eyes. But why did the gods not return? Had human beings somehow angered them, committed some fault that should be made good or repented? The toil in the desert was seen as a kind of 'sacrifice'. The more a person slaved away, the 'purer' he would seem in the eyes of the gods. The more impressive an earth marking appeared, the greater would be the gods' reward. This was also the reason why one tribe began to level the summit of one of the smaller mountains, and to scratch an ornamented runway out of the ground. It is a wonderful sight: the light strip on a darker background, with a kind of flower design emerging at its end.[101, 102] It was a particularly impressive invitation to the heavenly ones to land here rather than on a competitor's territory.

At some point people began to think they ought to tell the heavenly ones that they were expected and hoped for here on earth. The best way of doing this was to give a sign to heaven. Perhaps the chieftains also believed it was important to engrave their tribal symbols in a particularly lasting form into the ground, so that the heavenly ones would see them and bless their people. So the hard grind started all over again. Now the Indians carried stones away and began to scratch and scrape large areas. Ropes were laid out to guide this work. After the first tribal symbol had been completed – a spider – the artists among the Indians quickly noticed that the proportions were not right and that the curves were irregular. So they applied a simple method to improve the designs. With a wooden stick one of them etched a simple spider in the ground, no bigger than he could easily see at a glance. Then he laid small bright stones on his model, each stone representing a child. The children were called together and each one took up the position of one of the stones, though the children were spread out across the landscape on a much larger scale. They often had to be redirected because they weren't standing in the right place. But finally the wonder was achieved: a huge figure arose from a small model.

Whether it was like that or a little different we do not know. I am not even certain that the first, most ancient landing was by extra-terrestrials. Perhaps a vimana just flew by carrying human passengers, as described in ancient literature. But one thing is crystal clear to me: someone made a landing at some time, and then several more later on, otherwise landing-approach systems would not have been needed. Over many centuries the region became a cult site. The facts, engraved into the earth, prove it. And the reality of the runway on the Cordillera de Chicauma in Chile, at a height of 2,400 metres, proves that runway-building dates back to the very distant past.

The cat's-cradle network of lines also proves that many generations laid down signs that were different from their forefathers', often over the top of previous markings. One community might direct lines towards certain stars, while the next concentrated its artistry on the point of sunset at the beginning of autumn. If one tribe was content to make a narrow line of 900 metres, the next might think it should be 'endless', and culminate at a summit to serve the mysterious gods as an orientation point. And once one line had been drawn, the priests might consider that this was not enough, for tradition said that the gods had descended in heavenly chariots – which would make *two* furrows in the ground.

There is, let me say it again, no single, unifying system to be found at Nazca. The line and runway network is neither calendar nor map, neither cultural atlas nor astronomy book – and, naturally, no space-port either. There is no overall order, since each tribe and generation scratched different conceptions into the desert. And did this all begin because of prehistoric flights of some kind?

The figures on the mountain slopes make this clear – beings emanating rays, figures which point to the heavens with one arm and to the earth with the other. And not only in Nazca but from Chile to the southern USA as well. The same is true of the gods painted on ceramics and woven in cloth, which can be found all the way to Arizona – where to this day the Hopi Indians depict the heavenly visitors in the form of puppets. And let us not forget the deformed skulls, whether they belonged to actual 'gods' or were copied from them. If all this is not proof, if people are willing to ignore the facts in front of them, then a science based on gathering and collating information has lost its senses. But there are yet more indications to support my hypothesis.

Aeroplanes from ancient times

In the Gold Museum of the Colombian capital Bogota, aeroplane-like models that were found in royal graves have been on display for several decades. Archaeologists have interpreted them as insects, although an insect-cult is unknown throughout the whole of South America. These objects must have been connected with some cult, for otherwise they would not have been covered in valuable gold and laid in the graves of dead chiefs. Besides which, the wings of insects grow straight out from their bodies, rather than angled back like the aeroplane models in the Gold Museum. One such model has given rise to the logo of the Ancient Astronaut Society (AAS), an international organisation that concerns itself with traces left by extraterrestrials in the ancient past.

[103]

[104]

Now chance would have it that three close acquaintances of mine, Dr Algund Eenboom, Peter Belting and Conrad Lübbers, visited an exhibition of ancient Colombian jewellery in Bremen. These three are all members of the AAS and were therefore familiar with its logo. And there, among the exhibits, were some objects which closely resembled that logo. They had belonged 'to the Colombian collector, Vicente Restrepo from Medelin, who made them over to the Bremen business man Carl Schütte'.[11] In 1900, Schütte had donated about 4 kilos of gold treasure to what was then the Museum of Nature, Peoples and Trade in Bremen.

These aeroplane-like models have an unusual shape: large, high tail-fins, a pair of small rear wings, and a broad triangle of wings at the front. The nose is rounded, and just forward of where the large wings join is a wide opening, as though for a roomy cockpit. The thing actually looked incomplete. Could it possibly fly?

My three friends wanted to try this out. Peter Belting is a pilot himself; and so they started to make an exact replica of the AAS logo in the form of a larger-scale model aeroplane. The test flights exceeded all expectations,[103, 104] and represented a victory for pragmatic reason over academic prejudice. In spite of the 'cockpit hole' and the blunt nose, the model carried out every manoeuvre perfectly. And all this without any mechanical additions – such as landing aids or side rudders.

There is a postscript to this story. Five hours' drive from Santa Cruz in Bolivia, beside the little village of Samaipata, stands the mountain El Fuerte. Its peak resembles a pyramid, in whose slope are cut two parallel, straight grooves, 38 centimetres wide and 27 metres long. The highest point of the 'ramp' is formed by a circular form: a ring 2 metres in diameter on whose circumference are carved triangles and squares.[105, 106 – a model]

The experts have been puzzling over the significance of El Fuerte. Various ideas have been put forward, such as that it was an 'Inca cult site',[12] an 'ancestor cult' site,[13] the 'whim of a priest or a madman',[14] or some kind of military fortification. This last is the stupidest interpretation of all, for there was nothing to defend at El Fuerte. The mountain sits there like a man-made pyramid, open and accessible from all sides. A specialist in American studies, Dr Hermann Trimborn, [105

146

[106]

states that the whole complex was a 'unique creation, not comparable to any other ruins'.[15]

So how can we interpret this 'unique ruin'?

It no doubt served a cult of some kind, and cults are mostly connected with the gods. The 'cargo cults' of our century, though, come about when the advanced technology of one culture is misunderstood by another, technologically underdeveloped, culture. What cult was celebrated on the top of El Fuerte? Just imagine a model aeroplane, not of heavy gold as in Colombia, but built of lightweight wood. In theory this could have been covered in a fine layer of gold leaf, since South American cultures had mastered this technique long before the Incas. This aeroplane model is placed at the bottom of the ramp at El Fuerte and made fast on the occasion of a great festival.[107] Then a rubber band is attached to the model and pulled upwards to the ring with the carved triangles and squares at the summit. Oh yes, rubber was known in Central and South America long before the Europeans heard of it. At the upper end, the rubber band is wound around a wooden beam, and strong arms turn it around the centre of the ring. There, in the middle of the circle, there actually is a round lump of stone, part of the rock beneath. The more the rubber band stretches,

148

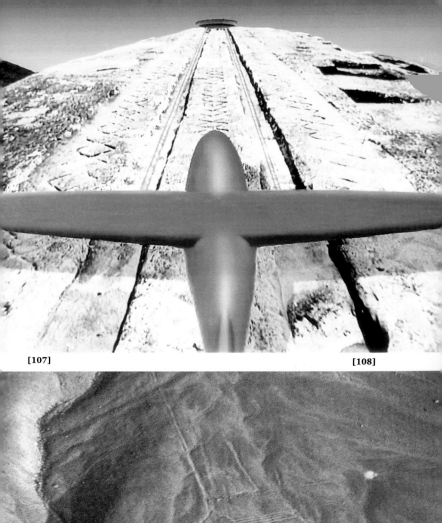

[107]

[108]

the harder the men have to pull. That is why they stop every now and then to rest, and anchor the beam in one of the carved squares. At the priest's command, someone cuts through the taut rubber band with one stroke of an axe, catapulting the model into the sky, towards the gods. It is also possible that small objects were placed in the plane as sacrificial offerings to the gods.

This is no more than an idea. Perhaps it can help to solve the riddle of El Fuerte. But what is certain is that there were aeroplane-type models in pre-Inca times, and that these have been shown to be perfectly airworthy. It is also certain that there existed in South and Central America a cult of the gods connected with flight. This is proven by Nazca and all the other places where drawings and figures are orientated towards the sky. There is even an 'aeroplane model' scraped out of the ground at Nazca – a 'bird' with rigid wings.[108]

But where did these gods come from? Were they after all human pilots from Asia who had developed more advanced technology than the South American Indians? Such differences between developed and undeveloped countries still exist today. But if so, where had the more advanced culture obtained its knowledge? From the gods, the heavenly teachers – according to ancient traditions. 'Pull the other one,' says the cynic, 'where can these extraterrestrials have come from, and, above all, how? And why?'

For the reasons I'll give you. Read on and find out.

Notes

1 F H Crick and L E Orgel, 'Directed Panspermia', *Icarus*, no. 19, London, 1983.

2 Erich von Däniken, *Habe ich mich geirrt?*, Munich, 1985.

3 Dileep Kumar Kanjihal, *Vimana in Ancient India (Aeroplanes or Flying Machines in Ancient India)*, trans. Julia Zimmerman, Bonn, 1991.

4 Lutz Gentes, *Die Wirklichkeit der Götter. Raumfahrt im frühen Indien*, Munich/Essen, 1996.

5 Erich von Däniken, *The Return of the Gods*, Element Books, Shaftesbury, 1997.

6 *Kebra Negest*, vol. 23, section 1, 'Die Herrlichkeit der Könige', treatises of the philosophical-philological class of the Royal Bavarian Academy of Sciences.

7 Berthold Laufer, 'The Prehistory of Aviation', *Field Museum of Natural History*, Anthropological Series, vol. 18, no. 1, Chicago, 1928.

8 Franz Bopp, *Ardschuna's Reise zu Indra's Himmel,* Berlin, 1824.

9 Erich von Däniken, *Der Götter-Schock*, Munich, 1992.

10 Protap Chandra Roy, 'Drona Parva', *The Mahabharata*, Calcutta, 1888.

11 Viola König, 'Die Wiederentdeckung des Goldes', *GEAS*, no. 5, October 1996.

12 Th. Herzog, *Vom Urwald zu den Gletschern der Kordilleren*, Stuttgart, 1913.

13 Leo Pucher, *Ensayo sobre el arte prehistorico de Samaipata,* San Francisco, 1945.

14 E Nordensköld, 'Meine Reise in Bolivien', *Globus*, vol. 97, 1910.

15 Hermann Trimborn, *Archäologische Studien in den Kordilleren Boliviens*, vol. 3, Berlin, 1967.

5

WHERE ARE THE EXTRATERRESTRIALS?

*Nothing in the world makes
people so afraid as the influence
of independent-minded people.*
ALBERT EINSTEIN, 1879–1955

On 8 August 1996, CNN broadcast a spectacular NASA press conference. NASA director Daniel Golden proudly announced that organic material had been discovered in a 3,500-million-year-old Mars meteorite. Or, to be more precise – traces of bacteria. The bacteria test was immediately given a scientific designation: ALH 84001. Several scientists explained how this discovery had been made and how they had managed to make the bacteria samples visible. Nine weeks later, Dr David McKay of the Johnson Research Center in Houston announced that new organic traces had been found in a Mars meteorite, one that was 'several thousand million years younger'.[1] The first analysis had been confirmed by a second – yet hardly anyone seemed interested. According to their ideological or religious inclination, people received the NASA announcement with either enthusiasm or shock. Traces of life on Mars? Unheard of! Aren't we alone in the endless reaches of the universe?

In the following weeks, opinions slowly crystallized in the daily papers, magazines and readers' letters. The Catholic Church had no fundamental objection to extraterrestrial life. God's Creation was, after all, infinite, and Jesus had said: 'In my Father's house are many dwellings.' Numerous sects, though, reacted quite differently. They believed that the Creation had taken place for Man's sake alone, and only Man could be redeemed by God's Son. It was an unbearable thought for them that somewhere out there in the universe might exist creatures who were not Christian and not burdened with Original Sin. Even more appalling was the idea that God might have sent His Son to countless other worlds, where the Crucifixion drama was endlessly replayed.

The scientific world remained sceptical and kept its cool for the time being. Then it began to respond through the media in the way one would have expected. Primitive life out there? Of course, why not? But only *primitive* life. Nobel Prize-winner Professor Dr Manfred Eigen said in the news magazine *Der Spiegel* that there was no reason why primitive single-cell life should have developed and produced more complex creatures. I quote: 'This is why we are highly unlikely to find higher life forms or even intelligence in the universe, at least not within our reach.'[2]

All nonsense, I would like to reply. We will find a wealth of intelligent life forms out there. Most of them will be similar to human beings; and travelling across interstellar distances will present absolutely no problem.

How can I publicly say such things? Is my assumption based on naive belief? On fantasy or self-opinionated stubbornness? Where is my proof?

For at least the last ten years every radio astronomer has known that the universe is full of the basic building blocks of life. These are in the form of molecule chains, and since every molecule has its own, typical vibration, its wavelength can be measured by our sophisticated giant radio-telescopes. That's happening all the time. Let me list just some of the well-known 'building blocks' that are swimming around the universe under the light pressure of some star or other:

chemical sign	molecule	wavelength
OH	Hydroxyl	18.0 cm
NH	Ammonia	1.3 cm
H_2O_3	Water	1.4 cm
H_2CO	Formaldehyde	6.2 cm
HCOOH	Formic acid	18.0 cm
H_3C-CHO	Acetaldehyde	28.0 cm

For life to develop, planets must orbit their sun at an ideal distance – their temperature must be neither too hot nor too cold. Since the Hubble Telescope has been searching the environment of certain stars, unhampered by disturbances from the earth's atmosphere, we have known with complete certainty that there are other planets beyond our own solar system. Steven Beckwith, director of the Max Planck Institute for Astronomy in Heidelberg believes that 'there is an abundance of planets in the galaxy', among them many with conditions favourable for life. And the British astronomer David Hughes adds: 'In theory at least there ought to be 60 billion planets orbiting in the Milky Way.' Four billion of these, he thinks, should be 'similar to earth, humid and with favourable temperature conditions'.[3] The statistical probability of finding earth-like planets was always going to be high. Suns are to planets as cats are to kittens.

Earth-like planets – and not only those – could be logically expected to contain water. NASA has discovered signs of water on the Jupiter moon Europa, frozen oxygen on the moon Ganymede, and ice in a moon crater. Even on Mars there is frozen water (ice) at the poles and below the surface. The idea that such extraterrestrial water is sterile will soon turn out to be wrong, for water always comes about in the same way. The planet cools, gases of all compositions are hurled up into the atmosphere, then rain down upon bubbling rock masses and turn once more to steam. Through millions of years the atoms bind together to form molecule chains, which in turn form – among other things – water. But this water flows, hisses and bubbles continually over and through stone formations, which already contain the components of life. The planets are, after all, all formed from the same basic material. What the radio astronomers receive as information from organic molecule chains in the cosmos, is also present in the crust of earth-like planets. There is no stone without minerals. The route to complicated chemical combinations, and from there to organic material, is the same in every case. Every chemistry student has known this since Stanley Miller made his experiments.

In 1952, the biochemist Dr Stanley Miller constructed a glass container in which he circulated an artificial atmosphere of ammonia, hydrogen, methane and water steam. To ensure that the experiment was conducted in wholly sterile conditions, Miller had first heated his apparatus and its contents for 18 hours at a temperature of 180 degrees Celsius. By means of two electrodes welded into the glass container, tiny primal storms were created. In a second glass sphere he heated sterile water whose steam flowed into the 'Miller apparatus' through a thin pipe. The cooled chemicals trickled back into the sphere of sterile water, were heated up and passed once more into the vessel containing the 'primal atmosphere'. In this way Miller created a continuous circulation – as had come about, so people then thought, at the creation of the earth. The experiment lasted for a week. At the end of it, the analyses showed the presence of amino butyric acid, aspartic acid, alanine and glycine – amino acids, in other words, which are necessary for the development of biological systems. In Miller's experiment, inorganic (dead) combinations had been transformed into complex organic substances.

In the following years, though, it is true, Miller was taken down a peg or two on occasion. The Nobel Prize-winners Francis Crick and James Watson discovered the double helix of DNA (deoxyribonucleic acid), which consisted of nucleotides without which no life would be possible. But Miller and his team quickly caught up. Changing the conditions of their experiment, they promptly found the presence of nucleotides. Nowadays it has become an accepted fact that the primal atmosphere cannot have consisted of hydrogen and methane, since sunlight would have decomposed them. But this knowledge only altered the substances in the experiment, and did not render it invalid.

For research chemists there is not the slightest doubt that organic combinations arise from inorganic ones. In the last 30 years, the Miller experiments have been repeated countless times and under varying conditions. Larger and larger amounts of amino acid have always been the result. Sometimes nitrogen was used instead of ammonia, sometimes formaldehyde or even carbon dioxide instead of methane. Miller's 'lightning' has sometimes been replaced by ultrasound or normal light. The results did not alter though. Each time, from each of these differently composed primal atmospheres containing no trace of organic life, amino acids and non-nitrogenous organic carbonic acids always arose. On some occasions the primal atmosphere even produced sugar.

Given this experimentally-deduced knowledge, and given the molecule chains discovered in the cosmos, I find it hard to understand why the NASA press conference caused so much fuss. Traces of life in the cosmos? What else would you expect? Organic substances in Mars rock? Of course! And what is true for Mars and the earth will hold good for all earth-like planets.

But organic molecules and primitive life forms like bacteria are of course a long way from complex life. Nobel Prize-winner Manfred Eigen is quite right in this respect. But for some reason our scientists have a strange tendency to restrict the development of complex life forms to earth alone. That is just egocentric! The miracle of humanity's evolution is supposed to have been possible *only here on earth*. Just how completely misguided this stubborn perspective is, is shown by the following conceptual experiment.

Johann von Neumann was a mathematician with fantastic ideas. In the fifties he dreamed up a strange machine, christened the 'von Neumann machine' by astronomers. This is always mentioned in specialist literature when there is any talk of making distant planets habitable, even though a 'von Neumann machine' has never been built.

The 'von Neumann machine' is a self-reproducing apparatus.[4] What does that mean?

A rocket-like machine takes off from the earth, leaves our solar system and heads for the next sun – Proxima Centauri, about four light years away. During the flight the apparatus puts out sensors to ascertain whether there are any planets orbiting around Proxima Centauri, and whether there is one within the ecosphere (ie, where conditions for life are possible). If there is no such planet the machine flies on, continuing its search for an earth-like planet. Once the von Neumann machine discovers a suitable planet, it steers towards it and effects a soft landing by means of a parachute.

On board the von Neumann machine are tools and extensions of all kind, various measuring instruments, a small blast furnace and a computer that directs the machine's activities. A miniature car is put down, feelers bore into the ground the strange world, the gas compositions are analysed, and of course a search is made to find out if there is any form of life. Step by step the von Neumann machine begins to make steel and iron, to form little cog-wheels and produce electricity. That all takes centuries, but the von Neumann machine has a great deal of time at its disposal. At some point or other, even if it takes 10,000 years, the von Neumann machine has fully reproduced itself and replaced the parts which were lost at the time of landing. Now there are two von Neumann machines. They both take off again from the strange planet, each taking as its goal a different sun. Over millions of years the von Neumann machines multiply and spread through a good proportion of the Milky Way – and go on doing so ad infinitum. The cost of the whole enterprise would be confined to the original machine.

Of course such a thing is unrealistic – Johann von Neumann himself knew this. Such an apparatus was a completely utopian idea in the fifties. And today?

In the past two decades computer technology has made advances which no one could have dreamed of in von Neumann's day. In the mid-eighties any PC worth its salt could manage a computational speed of one Megaflop (FLOPS = Floating Point Operations Per Second. Megaflops = a million Flops). Ten years later, the Gigaflop arrived (a thousand million Flops), and soon after that, ten Gigaflops were possible. Nowadays, 100 Gigaflop computers are used, and the Terraflop is being developed (a billion Flops). Insiders talk about the advent of 10 Terraflop computers. But at the same time as this development is taking place, the machines are also becoming smaller and smaller. The experts see no reason why a Terraflop computer couldn't be the size of a matchbox.

Another branch of technology that the public hears little about is 'nanotechnology'. A nanometre is one millionth of a millimetre – so small it's almost invisible. Yet it is possible to work at this microscopic scale and incorporate minuscule components. For example, at the Atomic Research Centre in Karlsruhe (Germany), a cogwheel made of nickel has been developed with a diameter of just 130 micrometres (one micrometre = 1,000 nanometres). Powered by air, the microscopic cog rotates 100,000 times per minute. And in various American technology institutes where 'nanotechnologists' are trained, there are micro-filters so tiny that bacteria get trapped in them. A great future is prophesied for such Lilliputian mechanics – for example in filtering gases, in microscopic robots and in medicine. Nanotechnology will soon be producing cardiac pacemakers, artificial pancreases, and 'nanocleaners' which travel through the blood system cleaning up furred arteries. It will create the tiniest possible electronic and mechanical apparatus, that can be applied in all sorts of situations.

This miniaturization in the world of computers and nanotechnology will allow the creation of von Neumann machines that are no bigger than a tennis ball, weighing no more than 100 grams. Even today, such 'tennis balls' could be catapulted from the moon or from one orbit to the next earth-like planet. They could attain speeds of up to 50 per cent of the speed of light and beam back their information to earth. And these von Neumann tennis balls would also reproduce themselves a good deal quicker than the old von Neumann concept allowed for. Although the public hasn't heard anything about it yet, there are various groups of space technologists who are giving serious thought to the matter.[5-7] And the cost? The NASA Apollo programme swallowed about 100 billion dollars. And at the moment the USA alone spends annually about 500 billion dollars on defence. In contrast, the cost of a miniature von Neumann machine would be negligible – for only the first one would cost anything.

If a von Neumann machine began to make copies of itself 50 years after reaching its first destination, these could then set off after another 50 years to new and further destinations. If we assume that the 'offspring' would set off to solar systems which are roughly 10 light years distant, then this would mean a speed of distribution of 10 light years every 60 years. Since our Milky Way extends for a distance of about 100,000 light years, colonization by von Neumann machines would take about 600,000 or 700,000 years. Or – depending on speed – twice or three times as long. Even if it took 10 million years, that would still be only a thousandth of the age of the Milky Way itself, for it has already notched up 10,000 million years.

But why send machines out into the cosmos when there is an easier way of going about it?

Like all living creatures the human being is 'a self-reproducing apparatus'. This 'apparatus' can be analysed right down to a single cell. Each cell contains the complete DNA necessary for developing the whole organism of the body. So why send complex technology into the far reaches of space if you can do exactly the same thing with microscopic DNA? Human DNA could be spread throughout the universe, either slowly or quickly. The slower version would involve catapulting small containers, hardly bigger than sewing needles, towards appropriate planets; or one could strew a particular section of the Milky Way with it – in the same kind of way that a farmer sows a field with corn. If the seed falls on unsuitable ground – sand, ice, rock or even water – it will not grow. If it falls on suitable soil it will be able to develop. All the information necessary for the corn to germinate is contained in its DNA.

One could be more specific in one's aim by shooting the DNA on a laser beam towards a particular, earth-like planet. This would start off an evolutionary process, just as happened on earth. And since the end result of this evolution would be intelligent human beings, they will also be inquisitive and sooner or later will ask: 'Where did we come from? Are we alone in the universe? How can we establish contact with other beings elsewhere? How can we spread ourselves through the cosmos?' They too will doubtless hit on the idea of the von Neumann machine, and reject it as surely as saying Amen at the end of a prayer. They will then discover their own DNA and see the light at last.

Our scientists, who keep saying that the distances in the cosmos are unbridgeable, that light years are a natural barrier, and that extraterrestrial life forms would never resemble human beings, have not yet seen the light. Their egocentricity prevents them from noticing what is obvious: the cosmos is bursting with life and human-like beings exist on other, earth-like planets. And this is so quite simply because they are all the offspring of an original species – about which we're not (yet) in a position to philosophize.

These ideas are not new, but they seem to be of hardly any interest to astronomers or even scientific journalists. At the end of the last century, the Swedish chemist and Nobel Prize-winner Svante August Arrhenius (1859–1927) postulated that life was eternal, irrespective of its origin. Naturally, he said, a circle has a beginning somewhere, but the moment the circumference meets itself and closes the ring, the question about its beginning is invalid – because it is unanswerable.

According to Arrhenius, all you can do is postulate a Creator – or whatever you understand by 'God' – at the beginning of the circle. I can only humbly accept this point of view.

Arrhenius also came up with the 'panspermia theory',[8] according to which the seeds of life are spread throughout the cosmos as automatically and naturally as dust spreads everywhere on the earth. Professor Fred Hoyle and the Indian professor N C Wickramsinghe, a mathematical genius, examined the panspermia theory and provided clear proof that seeds of life are disseminated throughout the universe via meteorites.[9] Every astrophysicist knows that planetary rock and comets are continually and without pause striking some planet or other in the universe. And the result? New bits of rock splinter off. When a meteorite hits the earth, rock is flung back into the cosmos, catapulted out beyond the gravitational field by the force of the impact. And what do such splinters of rock contain? The seeds of life of course! The dissemination of life across interstellar distances began thousands of millions of years ago. Whoever dismisses this idea is behaving like the proverbial ostrich.

Professor Francis Crick – a Nobel Prize-winner too, remember, not just some crackpot – went one step further. He suggested that an alien civilization might have shot micro-organisms into the universe thousands of millions of years ago with the help of spaceships, thus sowing the whole cosmos with life.[10]

After NASA had announced that primitive life had been discovered in a Mars meteorite, the question was raised whether it might not have been the other way round – whether perhaps, thousands of millions of years ago, a piece of earth rock had struck Mars and so planted earthly life there. 'Are we the Martians?' asked tongue-in-cheek journalists.

Such suggestions are typical – of course, life *must* have begun with *us!* But this doesn't get us any further. If the earth was the source of all life in the universe, then this must have happened 4,000 million years ago, for otherwise Mars could not, logically, have been 'fertilized' by the earth. And if Mars was fertilized in this way, then this could also have happened on other planets. Therefore we would – though unaware of it – have shot *our* seeds of life into the cosmos; and the question about how extraterrestrials could be 'terrestrial' would be void since we would share a common origin. But all this is just so much brain-torture, since life *cannot* have begun with us. As Hoyle and Wickramsinghe show beyond doubt, there was not enough time for this. If the earth, contrary to all likelihood, had really produced primitive life itself and *not* fertilized Mars, then this would mean that life had appeared twice and independently: on earth and on Mars. If this could happen twice in a small solar system like ours, then it must logically have happened a million times in the Milky Way.

In comparison to the rest of the Milky Way, let alone to other galaxies, the earth is a relatively young planet. Therefore on worlds which are thousands of millions of years older than ours, and which have thus had much more time to evolve, there must be no end of intelligent life. Since those older life forms were likely to have had an interest in disseminating themselves throughout the universe, we are similar to them – or they to us. Whichever way you look at it – panspermia theory or dissemination by means of intelligent extra-terrestrials – we cannot possibly be alone in the universe!

The specialist literature demonstrates that these conclusions are *not* the meanderings of a solitary nutcase.[11-15] Even 20 years ago, the astronomer James R Wertz worked out that extraterrestrials could easily have visited our solar system at intervals of 7.5 times 105 years – in other words, 640 times in the last 500 million years.[16] And 10 years later, Dr Martin Fogg of London University stated that many of the galaxies were probably already inhabited at the time our earth was taking shape.[17]

What, after all, do we really know in the midst of our splendid isolation? Science fiction postulates 'worm holes' which spaceships whizz through at many times the speed of light. Or 'space-time surfing'; or the 'warp-drive' so popular in TV series. These are all still in the realm of fantasy. But for how much longer? NASA has created a working group to give serious consideration to such ideas. The Breakthrough Propulsion and Power Working Group is connected to NASA's Advanced Space Transportation Programme, and is composed of a team of space scientists, physicists and astrophysicists. Their brief is to analyse the potential for such things, even if 'they contradict established theoretical opinion.'[18]

And those clever-dick astronomers who keep asking where these extraterrestrials are if they really exist, should be thankful to the ETs that they have some tact and circumspection in regard to us.

As I write these pages the world's press reports that the Vatican has, if 100 years late, finally recognized Darwin's theory of evolution as valid. In 1950 the Pope – Pius XII – in the encyclical *Humana generis* (On the Origin of Humanity), had said that Darwin's theory should be regarded as a hypothesis. Now Pope John Paul II has delivered a message to the Papal Academy of Sciences in which the theory of evolution has received the papal blessing. With astonishment one reads: 'New discoveries lead us to see more in the idea of evolution than only an hypothesis.' The Pope goes on to qualify this by saying that the theory of evolution is only relevant to the body: 'The soul is directly created by God.'[19]

According to this way of seeing things, the divine plan consisted of allowing 'chemical and physical processes to take their course'. The General Secretary of the Conference of Swiss Bishops, Nicholas Betticher, went into more detail:

God took care of the Big Bang, created stars, water, air and sun. This gave rise to the first cells, which developed further into amoebae, animals and finally human beings. The difference between humans and animals is the fact that God took a hand in evolution, breathed spirit into Man and created him according to His image.[20]

The clued-up theologians of the Roman church don't seem to have noticed that this blows the biblical story of Creation to smithereens. What is left of the Original Sin committed in Paradise if evolution follows the Darwinian model? And why do we need 'redemption' by 'God's Son' if the Fall never took place?

Anyway, it wasn't God who created the human being 'in His image', but 'the gods', in the plural. That's also how it reads in the Hebrew original of the first book of Moses. (The word 'Elohim' that is used in Genesis is actually a plural concept.) If we just replace the little word 'gods' with 'extraterrestrials' we've finally hit the nail on the head. But this will not be accepted until the ETs land on St Peter's Square in

Rome and celebrate a service in honour of all Creation. At which point, perhaps, we'll get the encyclical *Ad honorem extraterrestris* (In Honour of the Extraterrestrials).

Blasphemy? – Oh, rubbish! After all, at the beginning of the chain of Creation stands the grandiose spirit underlying the whole universe. Or, in other words, God.

Notes

1 'Wieder Spuren von Leben in Stein vom Mars entdeckt', *Welt am Sonntag*, no. 41, 6 October 1996.

2 'Die Funde passen ins Bild', *Der Spiegel*, no. 33, 1996.

3 'Planeten-Brut aus dem Urnebel', *Der Spiegel*, no. 22, 1993.

4 Arthur W Burks, *Theory of Self-Reproducing Automata by John von Neumann*, University of Illinois Press, 1966.

5 Georg von Tiesenhausen and Wesley A Darbo, *Self-Replicating System – A System's Engineering Approach*, NASA Technical Memorandum TM-78304, Marshall Space Flight Center, Alabama, July 1980.

6 Jacqueline Signorini, 'How a SIMD machine can implement a complex cellular automation. A case study of von Neumann's 29-state cellular automation', *Super Computing 89*, ACM Press, 1989.

7 Richard D Klafter, Thomas Chmielewski and Michael Negin, *Robotic Engineering: An Integrated Approach*, Prentice Hall, 1989.

8 F H Crick and L E Orgel, 'Directed Panspermia', *Icarus*, no. 19, London, 1973.

9 Fred Hoyle and N C Wickramsinghe, *Die Lebenswolke*, Frankfurt/Main, 1979.

10 Francis Crick, *Das Leben selbst. Sein Ursprung, seine Natur*, Munich and Zurich, 1981.

11 Ralph C Merkle, 'Molecular Nanotechnology', *Frontiers of Supercomputing – II: A National Reassessment*, University of California Press, 1992.

12 Ralph C Merkle, 'Two Types of Mechanical Reversible Logic', *Nanotechnology*, vol. 4, 1983.

13 Erik K Drexler, *Molecular Engineering: an approach to the development of general capabilities for molecular manipulation*, National Academy of Sciences, USA, 1978, pp. 5275–8.

14 Ralph C Merkle, 'A Proof About Molecular Bearings', *Nanotechnology*, vol. 4, 1993, pp. 86–90.

15 Ralph C Merkle, 'Self-Replicating Systems and Molecular Manufacturing', *Journal of the British Interplanetary Society*, vol. 45, 1992, pp. 407–13.

16 James R Wertz, 'The Human Analogy and the Evolution of Extraterrestrial Civilisations', *Journal of the British Interplanetary Society*, vol. 29, no. 7/8, 1976.

17 Martin J Fogg, 'Temporal Aspects of the Interaction among the First Galactic Civilisations. The Interdict Hypothesis', *Icarus*, vol. 69, 1987.

18 Johannes Fiebag, 'Völlig abgehoben?', *Ancient Skies*, no. 6, 1966.

19 'Der Mensch stammt doch ab', *Focus*, no. 44, 1966.

20 'Yes to Darwin – but God took care of the Big Bang', interview by Susanne Stettler, *Der Blick*, 28 October 1996.

APPENDIX –
FASCINATING NAZCA

The photographs numbered 109 to 124 are additional pictures of Dr Cabrera's collection in Ica, Peru. Photographs 125 to 144 are details of the Nazca region which are not mentioned in the text. There are always new and exciting or puzzling things to be discovered!

[109]

[110] △   △ [111]

[112] ▽

47

[125]

[126]

[127]

[128]

[132]

178

[134]

[135]

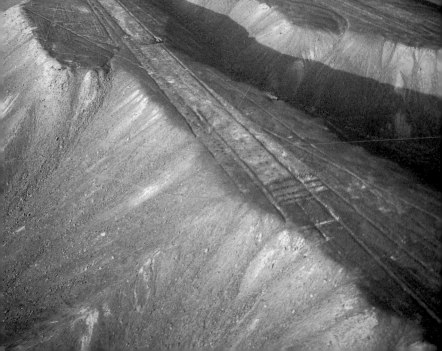

[136]

[137]

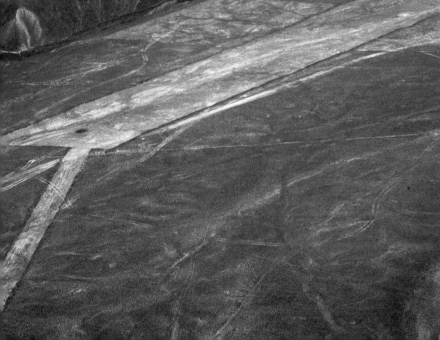

[138]

[139]

[140]

[141]

[142]

[143]

[144]

DEAR READER...

A non-fiction book is different from a novel. Of course the non-fiction writer can also fantasize a bit and certainly theorize – but he must first do his research. This can take years and cost a lot of money. Neither flights nor camera equipment are free, and offices and assistants have to be paid for.

So I count myself lucky to have friends who are always ready to lend a selfless hand. There is Uli Dopatka, librarian at the University of Bern, who has supplied me with masses of literature on the subject. And Valentin Nussbaumer who, together with Uli, assisted me at Dr Cabrera's house and in Nazca for weeks on end. Nor do I want to forget Peter Kaschel, a graduate teacher in Recklinghausen. He has the courage to discuss the controversial theme of 'Däniken' at the secondary school where he teaches. He also proofread my manuscript. And then there are my good friends Dr Eenboom, Peter Belting and Conny Lübbers, who gave a lot of their time to build and test a model aeroplane based on an ancient design. Then my secretary Kilian Bohren, who quickly found his feet in my office and has long since got used to dealing with its daily whirl of demands, with or without my presence. And last but not least, my wife Elisabeth, who has much patience and understanding for my work, although it means that I am so seldom at home.

My gratitude to them all is heartfelt, not prompted by politeness or duty.

Nazca is just *one* of the great riddles of our world. There are others, on all five continents, but they are accessible only to a few. Only a small proportion of humanity can make journeys to distant lands, visit humid jungles or head for arid desert places. There is still a great deal for the youth of today to discover – but first you have to ask the right questions.

We would like to offer as many people as possible the chance of studying the great riddles of the world, in a living, three-dimensional, interactive context. That's why we are planning a theme park, to be built over the next few years in Interlaken in the Bern mountains. A foundation has been set up, and a project group is working on the idea. Find out how *you* can get involved by sending off for a free detailed prospectus. Just write to Erich von Däniken at CH-3803 Beatenberg, Switzerland.

With best wishes,

Erich von Däniken

Picture credits

Valentin Nussbaumer, Zurich: 27, 28, 29, 44, 45, 52, 66, 67, 114, 123, 124
Willi Dünnenbaumer, Quito: 83, 89
Torsten Sasse, Berlin: 85–89
Jaime Bascur, Santiago de Chile: 90
All other photographs by Erich von Däniken, Beatenberg.

INDEX